from

PEASANT FOODS

to

SUPERFOODS

from
PEASANT FOODS
to
SUPERFOODS

MELISSA GEARING

ISABELLA MEDIA INC.
NEWPORT, RI
www.isabellamedia.com

Eat well and be well.

Sign up today to get naturopathic and nutrition Skype appointments, access to a detox program, newsletter, and cutting-edge information on health, wellness, fitness, and living your life to the fullest.

Visit Melissa online at www.mgherbs.com

Mention of specific companies, organizations, or authorities in this book does not imply endorsement by the author or publisher, nor does mention of specific companies, organizations, or authorities imply that they endorse this book, its author, or the publisher.

Internet addresses and telephone numbers given in this book were accurate at the time it went to press.

Copyright © 2019 Isabella Media Inc

All rights reserved. No parts of this book may be used or reproduced in any manner whatsoever without written permission from the author, except in case of brief quotations embodied in critical articles and reviews.

PRINTED IN THE UNITED STATES OF AMERICA

Book design by Isabella Book Design

Library of Congress Cataloging-in-Publication Data is on file with the publisher.

ISBN-13: 978-1-7330416-1-4

Follow us

@isabella_media

CONTRIBUTORS

My contributors are all local, female entrepreneurs out there working hard to sell themselves and build a little—or big—business, just like me. They are artists at what they do and always the professional. They have been so supportive and extremely patient with me. There would be no book without them! An exceptional thanks to Elise who is brilliant and talented; who converts my crazy ongoing ideas into logical print form and takes all my calls and emails seriously despite the ever-changing demands. Each of these ladies has become a valued friend in the stressful and all-consuming process of cookbook creation.

Elise Lewerenz
Food Stylist & Graphic Designer
Peachy Art + Design - www.peachydesign.co | @peachyartndesign

Erin Brooks
Photographer & Food Stylist
Erin Brooks Photographer - @erinbrooksphotographer

Cindra Banks
Media & Promotions

Miriam Ragen
Food Stylist
MIM Concepts - www.mimconcepts.com.au | @mimconcepts

Sophie Tyler
Food Photographer
Sophie Tyler Photography - www.sophietylerphotography.com | @sophietylephotography

A special thanks to **Jacquie Garcia** of Leiluca Ceramics who was kind enough to let us use some of her beautiful pottery for the photos. Shop these pieces and more at *www.etsy.com/au/shop/leiluca*

CONTENTS

INTRODUCTION X
MY STORY XIII
LET'S PREP XVI
SUPERFOOD GLOSSARY . . . XVIII

1

PART ONE | SUPERCHARGED RECIPES
FERMENTS & PICKLING 3
BRAISING, BOILING & BROTHING . . 37
OFFAL—IS NOT AWFUL 63
GUT GOLD 81
BLEND IT 99
SUPER SIDES. 117

2

PART TWO | EVERYDAY FAMILY MEALS
RISE & SHINE 161
LUNCH BREAK 181
THE MAIN EVENT 201
SWEET NOTHINGS 225

3

PART THREE | HOMEMADE STAPLES
LSA 240
CHIA SEED EGGS 240
TOMATO BASE SAUCE 243
CAULIFLOWER RICE 243
WHIPPED COCONUT CREAM . . .244
RANCH DRESSING 244
HOMEMADE MAYO 246

HINTS FOR HEALTHY COOKING. 249
A QUICK GUIDE TO SUGAR 249
A QUICK GUIDE TO OILS 250
IN-THE-KITCHEN RECOMMENDATIONS . . . 250
HEALTHY CONDIMENT OPTIONS 250
THE MGHERBS 1 WEEK DETOX 253
ACKNOWLEDGEMENTS 263
INDEX 264

INTRODUCTION

I should start by saying I am no chef. This book has come about through my journey with food and food intolerances and the need to share this information with my clients who were experiencing similar things. It started to grow and expand when I realized that there was a gigantic gap in what people thought was healthy and what we know is healthy, what we are being told for financial gain and what is the truth for our best health.

One of the biggest obstacles that people face when trying to change their diet is the onslaught of opinions about good and bad food. I believe there is no 'good' nor 'bad' food. Sure, there are some imposters on our supermarkets' shelves pretending to be food, but when you stick to whole real food, there are no enemies. The key to a balanced diet is moderation, not avoidance or restriction and merely eating the real, seasonal food that nature has gifted us.

I do not have time for strict fad diets, extremism or dogmatism. What I want to share is the everyday food, to educate people that life is not all or nothing, it is a constant balance. An effort and a choice to maintain equilibrium-and that means eating cake at the party sometimes and enjoying a drink. I come from a genuine place when I give advice. I believe in what I tell my clients. I believe it is the best way to live a healthy life. I practice what I preach, and I preach what I practice-I do not believe in giving a false sense of perfectionism.

I want to educate people on the way to live a simple and balanced life through the food and medicine we have been surrounded by in our environment. I believe this is the key to good health, happy minds and managing chronic conditions effectively. I hope you can use the recipes in this book and that some may even hold a coveted space on your weekly meal planner for the family.

MY STORY

In 2014, I went to Bali for a friend's wedding and brought a parasite home with me. After a year and no luck killing it I was sickly, underweight, depressed and suffered constant stomach troubles, migraines, and fatigue. When I finally succumbed to antibiotics (literally my life saver), I was left with eleven food intolerances and a journey of discovery as to what anaphylactic allergies I had developed.

My diet was limited but as fellow foodies will know this does little to diminish a passion for food. And so, I started to adapt recipes and get creative in the kitchen. At first, I made complicated and expensive meals with gluten and dairy free alternatives, egg replacer and faux foods. However, I soon got tired of needing an assortment of special foods to make dinner or whip up a treat for the weekends.

From this came a return to real food (with my twist) and a return to healthy well-balanced meals. Many gluten-free options are high in refined starches and sugar, many dairy alternatives are full of soy or sugar, and something like egg replacer suddenly seemed ridiculous. Why not use a banana, some chia seeds or psyllium husk to hold a cake or meatball together? Using food as food and adding nutrition at the same time.

I found myself going back to recipes that my Grandparents had taught me and made for me as a child. Stews, casseroles and slow cooker meals, roasts, braised meats, and curries. Eating slow cooked meals and including offal where I could, meant that I could access an array of nutrients which were already broken down so my poor tummy could absorb them. All naturally free from inflammatory foods, filling, homey and packed with fat, protein, and nutrition.

My years in health food made it easy for me to start to replace simple things like nuts with seeds, eggs with chia eggs and milk with a range of seed milks and coconut milk. Along the way, I learned the value of fermented foods and developed skills in doing this at home, which I now teach all my clients and anyone else who is interested. In addition to tasting great and adding new flavors to my palate, fermented foods were vital to healing the damage done to my gut by the parasite.

And then there are my clients. If I thought I had it bad, I had no idea. The tummy troubles that some people struggle with are shocking. Do we think it's normal? Or is it because we have been given the diagnosis of IBS we believe there is nothing more to be done? From chronic diarrhea to chronic constipation, bloating and pain after eating and then fatigue, depression, and anxiety that this can cause.

I will never forget the lady who had suffered terribly with chronic stomach trouble since childhood, swinging bowels, urgency, weight gain, sharp pains and severe bloating. Only to be told there was nothing wrong and nothing to be done. She just had IBS. Working together for the last three years, she is now healthy, fit, strong and well with absolutely no stomach or bowel complaints. I could not be happier or prouder of all her hard work. We have now started to successfully reintroduce some of the foods which had previously caused her pain.

As I started to find wellness again and develop a tolerance to reintroduce foods, I wanted to share this way of healing through food. Of course, I am an herbalist, and I use herbs and supplements as well to help heal the gut but this is short-term, and the goal is always to help the body find normality again. Food is long-term medicine, lifestyle change and re-working how you think about food is essential.

Rather than new ideas, I find myself preaching old ways of eating and enjoying food that we have moved away from and lost throughout the many years of fat-free, sugar-free, low carb, fad dieting. This way of eating involves going back to our roots and how our ancestors ate. I could then integrate my knowledge of healthy foods and utilize the best offerings of the superfood movement.

To me, all whole foods are superfoods. Whole foods are foods that come just as they are and have been, for the best part, unchanged. Think fruit, vegetables, nuts, seeds, grains, and many animal products. The study of nutrition and implementing a balanced way of cooking and eating really took me back to my childhood and what my grandparents cooked, ate and shared with me. Reintroducing butter and throwing away margarine, saving the lard from the cooking process and learning to prepare, cook and eat new (and old) parts of each animal.

Moving away from fast food cooking and towards slow cooking, braising, and pressure cooking allows so much more nutrients to be transferred from the food to our bodies plus gives such a better flavor. It is also an excellent way to eat for leaky gut and an easy way for kids to enjoy tougher cuts of meat. A bonus is that when we eat this way we save money. By eating cuts that are not as popular and using the whole animal, we get better yield (so we can feed more people) and we do not pay a premium. It is cheaper to buy one whole chicken than a few kilos of chicken breast. This allows us to afford better quality meat and move away from mass-produced, feedlot animals and to stop supporting such industries.

My favorite part of all of this is being transported to my Grandad's kitchen as a child whenever I smell offal cooking, such as kidneys or liver. Many people will screw their nose up at the idea of eating offal, but as you read through the book hopefully you will see the beauty that I do in using these incredibly nutritious and delicious parts, and maybe even try them. Starting with something as simple as a steak and kidney pie is a great way to introduce new flavors to the family in a familiar and tasty way.

Eat well and be well.

LET'S PREP

All real foods are SUPER foods. The key word here is real. Real, whole foods are medicine, and they all possess innate abilities to serve our bodies and communicate with our cells in their unique way. There have been many foods in the last few years that have been touted as superfoods, and it has become a word associated with expensive, hard to pronounce and alternative health foods. However, we have always known that oats give us energy and beetroot makes us poop. We may just not have known exactly why, and we didn't think of them as super- they are just everyday foods that we eat to help keep us full and make us feel like we can face the day. There is a vast difference between margarine and butter. One is real food, and one has been dreamed up in a lab and has a beautiful yellow color added in the end to make it resemble its counterpart.

Here are descriptions of some of the fantastic superfoods that are used in the book, and some extras to get you started. One of my aims in writing recipes is to ensure that you can whip something up at home out of everyday ingredients. Do not underrate the power of your meat and veg combinations. However, some extra little things can make it easier for you to get more nutrients and they become especially important if you are unwell or trying to achieve a health goal.

If you have any gut complaint, from a leaky gut to food allergies & intolerances, it can be as simple as adding some good quality gelatin to your pantry. Once you are comfortable with using this, you may like to try some hemp seeds in a smoothie. Whatever you do, don't feel like you have to have a health food shop at home. Just start with a few little things, allow them to become the norm (if you like them), and add to your journey as you go. If you don't like it, there is no need to force it down or upon the kids. As you can see there are many different superfoods and this list is indeed not exhaustive. Many of the properties also overlap so get through the bag or give it away if you do not like it and try something different next time.

SUPERFOOD GLOSSARY

ALMONDS are high in magnesium, calcium, protein and good fats. These super nuts are the perfect addition to the diet for recovery. They also keep you full and help stabilise blood sugar levels as they are slow burning fuel for your body. A tasty addition to an afternoon fruit or veg snack to help make the energy from other foods last longer.

ACAI is full of anthocyanins, flavonoids, anti-aging pigments, lot's of minerals and vitamins, as well as omega-3, 6 and 9. It is a super powerful berry and is loaded with 19 amino acids, 30% fibre, and monosaturated fats. It also has low GI and low sugar, making it a heart-healthy essential.

BANANA is rich in potassium but what does that mean? It means that they can help reduce high blood pressure and risk of stroke as potassium helps to stop hardening of the arteries. Banana can also help reduce reflux as its works like an antacid so is great for gut healing. They are also jammed with energy so are perfect for a pre-workout snack or if you are just on the go and need a pickup. A perfect component of an energy smoothie!

BEETROOT is full of nitric oxide, which relaxes the blood vessels and increases oxygen circulation in the blood. It is perfect for those with high blood pressure. Beetroot is also great for detoxifying the liver so it can assist with weight loss goals and cleansing. As a vasodilator it can also be used as nature's Viagra for the boys.

CARROT is full of the powerful antioxidant beta carotene which is super important for good skin, so it will help to clear any blemishes and also supports your immune system. Carrots also reduce your risk of heart disease and cancer with this amazing antioxidant, fighting free radicals in the body. Of course, it's still great for eyesight as we all know as well!

CHIA seed is the ultimate seed and is thought to be the most nutritious food in the world. We now grow the majority of chia here in Australia in the Kimberleys. Full of omega 3, 6 and 9, antioxidants, protein, calcium, protein, magnesium and fibre, these little miracle seeds are anti-inflammatory, blood sugar balancing, satiating and great for detoxing the gut and bowels. Easy to throw into a smoothie or sprinkle on top of salads.

CACAO is a natural antidepressant and stress reliever! Cacao is full of antioxidants which keep our mind sharp and our skin young. Plus it's the highest magnesium food in the world which is important in preventing cramps and headaches (hence why we girls crave it around our cycles!) as well as helping with stress and anxiety. It is the most mineral rich superfood, and is energizing and mood enhancing since it increases serotonin levels in the brain (our feel good chemical). It has almost double the ORAC value (Oxygen Radical Absorbance Capacity) as acai berry and is rich in polyphenols to help reduce cholesterol and support heart health.

COCONUT is the ultimate fat. It keeps us full, satiated and helps stabilize blood sugar levels as it is slow burning fuel for your body. Coconut is also antimicrobial so is perfect for keeping any nasty bugs at bay. It will help keep your mind switched on fighting brain fog and is great for your hair, skin and nails as well!

COCONUT OIL is a rich source of super good saturated fats (90%) which are medium chain triglycerides. This means that they are metabolized uniquely and can actually help to burn fat when eaten by increasing the calories you burn. This oil is also antimicrobial so can help kill pathogens in the body and on the skin as well. It will keep you full and reduce hunger and sugar cravings.

FLAXSEED/LINSEED are the same thing! These little seeds are full of oily fibre which is a prebiotic, and they assist the bowels to move well. They also provide a beautiful balance of omega 3 and protein, as well as many micronutrients, and are one of the oldest seeds in the world.

GINGER is warming, encouraging the blood to move around the body. It is also anti-inflammatory and can assist with pain, cramps, cold hands and feet, and arthritis. A little ginger each day can assist in healing a leaky gut as well.

GOJI BERRY is the ultimate berry! They are unlike any other berry as they are full of protein, including 18 essential amino acids. Plus more beta carotene than our carrot friends, high vitamin C, B2, A, iron and selenium. Gojis are also full of antioxidants which are great for the skin and in preventing cancer.

GOLDEN BERRIES are full of vitamin A, vitamin C, fibre and calcium. They have a high protein count and are a good source of bioflavonoids (vitamin P). Gobble these straight up, or add to trail mix, fruit cakes, muffins and more.

HEMP is full of chlorophyll, all 8 essential amino acids, essential fatty acids-omega 3 and gamma-linolenic acid. High in iron, magnesium and zinc, it is a great source of plant protein. It is easy to digest and is alkaline to help balance hormones, as well as provides full amino acid profile, is high in minerals, and easy to absorb. Note: hemp seeds DO NOT contain THC.

HIMALAYAN SALT is an amazing substitute for avoiding refined salt. This is most important due to the additions of nasty chemicals and bleaching that can be found in your average table salt. Pink salt helps to balance electrolytes in the body so that you hydrate better while providing a huge array of micronutrients. It also has healing properties and is known for its effect on allergies, sinus and asthma. It aids in nutrient absorption and helps to reduce fluid retention, and maintains an acid-alkaline balance in the body. Plus it contains over 84 minerals!

KALE will assist with liver detox and fat metabolism, like most leafy greens. It also has the added benefit of being jammed with so many nutrients that it has been dubbed a superfood in its own right. It is full of vitamins and minerals including the ever elusive and always needed magnesium.

LUCUMA contains carbohydrates, fibre, vitamins, and minerals. It is loaded with antioxidants such as beta carotene and complex carbs, fibre, B3, zinc, magnesium and iron. With a creamy citrus flavor, not only does it smell delicious, it can also be used as a low GI subtle sweetener and as a natural flavoring.

MACA is high in iron, iodine, calcium, magnesium, phosphorus, potassium, zinc, selenium, and vitamins B1, B2, C, and E. It is full of amino acids and plant sterols which improve immune system and lower cholesterol. Maca is an energy food, and a powerful adaptogen. It can help enhance energy without being a stimulant. It is also able to increase libido and energy, and help decrease chronic fatigue, anxiety and stress, as well as enhancing fertility by normalizing the hormones testosterone, progesterone and estrogen. Perfect in smoothies with nuts and seeds, and sweet fruits like banana and dates due to its malty, earthy flavor that varies from butterscotch to radish-like depending on what it is accompanying.

MAQUI contains anthocyanins, antioxidant levels 3 times higher than acai, has higher ORAC (Oxygen Radical Absorbance Capacity) levels than any other fruit discovered, is high in vitamin C, low in sugar, and one for one contains 10 times the amount of antioxidants in a blueberry. Add it to smoothies, juices, cereals, water, and yoghurt. It has a mild flavor and cannot be tasted in smoothies but gives a vibrant and intense violet color.

MESQUITE has a great mineral profile including significant calcium and magnesium, high lysine, low GI (25), and high protein, making it a wonderful diet addition to keep full for

longer or help with muscle recovery. It can also be used to assist weight loss by adding it to shakes.

QUINOA is high in lysine, manganese, magnesium, potassium, phosphorus, copper, zinc, vitamin E and B6, riboflavin, niacin and thiamine. This little grain has more calcium than milk, as well as antioxidants, fibre, and iron. It is high in unsaturated fats, low carb and low GI. Quinoa is a complete food and high in protein, full of vitamins, gluten/wheat free, and cholesterol free. Quinoa grains make a perfect substitute for rice, quinoa flakes can be used in place of oats, and quinoa flour is wonderful for gluten-free baking.

SPIRULINA is nature's multi vitamin. Spirulina is jam packed with nutrients and helps the body to detox any heavy metals, as well as kill off any pathogenic bugs. It also improves energy and may assist with weight loss as is it so nutrient-dense.

TURMERIC is the ultimate anti-inflammatory food! Turmeric works in every part of the body to reduce inflammation. It can also move out excess fluid and encourages huge detoxing from the liver so that all toxins are sent out of your body. This may assist with weight loss goals as well.

VEGETABLE PROTEIN POWDER. Although I am the biggest fan of a real food approach, I do believe that good quality food based protein powder has a place. Rather than get pea or rice or another type of single plant-based protein, look for a blend. Protein is essentially a chain of links we call amino acids. When we look at amino acids from animal sources such as eggs and meat, they are complete. This means they have all of the links in the chain. Plant proteins are often incomplete, missing a link or two. This means that they do not serve the body with a whole protein and therefore do not function as well in the body. This is why teaming foods together is essential for vegetarians or adding an animal product such as cheese or milk. Combining the right foods will deliver a complete protein from plant bases, such as eating almonds, brazil nuts, and cashews altogether. This can be done with plant protein powder as well. By using rice and pea protein, and adding some extra goodies such as chia and linseeds, it is a rich protein source. This is a much more natural source of protein for the body to utilize than whey protein powder.

Part 1
Supercharged Recipes

Chapter 1
FERMENTS & PICKLING

Fermenting food is like pre-digesting it for our gut. When we eat it, it is super easy to breakdown and our tummy has less work to do. This increases the bio-availability of the nutrients in the food and allows us to better absorb all of the vitamins and minerals.

It also does this for whatever food we eat with it. It's a good idea to have a little fermented food with each meal, or at least once per day. Fermenting food has become trendy and popular due to the movement to better the state of our gut. This is due to the high amounts of good bacteria in properly fermented food and drinks. It is these good bacteria that do most of the work in a fermentation process. Good quality fermented food will have a similar effect in our bodies to that of probiotics.

Fermenting also preserves the food we are using and it originated for this reason, before there was access to refrigeration. Food would be harvested in its peak, prepared and jarred for fermentation, and stored for the winter time when it was no longer abundant.

For all ferments it is important to use filtered water and always wash your hands before starting. It is even a good idea to throw a bit of vinegar over your hands before starting to massage cabbage or when handling your scoby.

The ferment will eat most of the sugar that you feed it, as you become more confident with fermenting you may be able to get away with less sugar but keep in mind your culture will die if it does not have enough to eat.

sauerkraut

Plain old-fashioned sauerkraut is always the easiest place to start when you begin your fermenting journey. It is so easy in fact that all you really need to source is a cabbage. There are varying species of naturally occurring bacteria on cabbage leaves which make it the perfect fermenting vegetable. These include some of the common bugs seen in probiotics such as Lactobacillus species. For the little guys to do their job they need an anaerobic environment, which is why we seal the cabbage in a jar. Over time, the bacteria produce carbon dioxide and the acidic environment means that only the good bugs survive. These are the ones that we want to colonies our gut.

INGREDIENTS

- 1 cabbage head of your choice
- Himalayan crystal salt (fine)
- Water if needed
- Juniper berries
- Jar with lip lock lid and rubber seal

METHOD

Slice cabbage roughly. Add 3-4 handfuls of salt to start. Strongly massage the cabbage with your hands until it starts to get soft and break down. It should start to leak a watery substance. If it is not softening after a few good squeezes, add more salt (you can also taste your cabbage to determine if it needs more salt or not).

When the cabbage is soft, floppy, and wet, mix in your juniper berries or any other spice you like. Some ideas include black peppercorns, fennel seeds or something adventurous like spirulina powder.

Start to pack it tightly into a glass jar with a clip lock lid and a rubber seal. Fill your jar with 5cm of space at the top.

Check it daily and refrigerate when it gets to your desired taste in order to halt the fermentation process.

kimchi

Kimchi is a must-have side dish that is on every table in Korea and Japan. It is rich in fibre, vitamin A, vitamin C, thiamine (B1), riboflavin (B2), calcium, and iron, and also contains many beneficial lactic acid bacteria.

INGREDIENTS

- 1 head Chinese cabbage
- ¼ cup Himalayan salt
- 5 to 6 cloves of garlic (pickled if you'd like)
- A large knob of ginger
- 2 tablespoons fish sauce
- 1 tablespoon seaweed flakes (wakame, kelp)
- 1-5 tablespoons Gochugaru (Korean red pepper flakes from an Asian grocer)
- 1 daikon, peeled and cut into matchsticks
- ½ bunch of shallots, sliced
- 4 carrots, grated
- Jar with clip lock lid and rubber seal

METHOD

Slice the cabbage into thick strips (core if you wish). Place the cabbage and salt in a large bowl. Use your hands to massage together until soft and watery. Combine garlic, ginger, soy sauce, seaweed and Gochugaru in a bowl. You can use 1 tablespoon of spice for mild or 5 if you like it hot.

Put gloves on and add daikon, carrots and shallots to the cabbage in a large bowl and coat with sauce mix. Mix with hands to coat. Pack it tightly into a clip lock jar with a rubber seal. Press down so the brine rises and covers cabbage.

You may need to add a small amount of water to cover but it will make a lot of its own liquid as well. Leave an inch of head-space and seal it shut. Check it daily and refrigerate when it gets to your desired taste in order to halt the fermentation process.

misomite

Whenever I run fermentation workshops I save this one for last. It is the easiest thing to do but is always the favourite and the one that makes it home first. This spread delivers everything you want from a morning started with Vegemite on toast, only you now have a wheat free, preservative free version. Misomite is also packed with naturally occurring minerals and is high in calcium. Miso is full of enzymes and also contains a complete protein (see the glossary for more on protein) so will keep you full for longer than many commercially made breakfast spreads.

INGREDIENTS

- Tahini paste (get black tahini if you want it to look like Vegemite)
- Miso paste (refrigerated section at Asian grocer)

METHOD

Mix equal amounts of tahini and miso together and taste. Add more tahini if it is a little too 'yeasty' tasting.

TO USE

Enjoy misomite as a spread; pair with some sliced avocado and cracked pepper on toast for an easy brekkie. Add some olive oil, red wine vinegar, cracked pepper, and a dash of maple syrup to a few tablespoons of misomite to make a yummy salad dressing. Use it to flavor stir-fries or steak when cooking.

cultured carrot

Carrot is a superfood. You only have to look at its vibrant color to know that it is good for you. Food has an innate ability to attract us when it is good for us, and disgust us when it is bad. If we are in balance we can see, smell and feel Mother Nature's message through the food that has been given to us. This is certainly becoming harder as more food is processed and packaged and its origins and nature are more difficult to decipher. The average garden carrot should not be underestimated, but we can power it even more by fermenting it. Cultured vegetables are some of the most potent and ultimate superfoods. By culturing the carrot, it allows the gut to absorb more nutrients including all of the minerals and B vitamins. Carrot is also one of the best ferments to start the kids on as it is sweet and colourful.

INGREDIENTS

- 6 carrots
- 2 tablespoons wakame flakes (seaweed optional)
- 3 tablespoons sesame seeds
- 3 tablespoons pepita seeds
- 3 teaspoons of Himalayan salt
- Fresh cracked pepper to taste
- 1 teaspoon food probiotics
- 3-4 cups of fresh filtered water
- Jar with clip lock lid and rubber seal

METHOD

Grate the carrots into a large bowl. Add the seaweed flakes, seeds and salt and pepper, plus the probiotics. Add 1 cup of water and start to massage the carrot with your hands.

Start to put the carrot into the jar, punching it down as you go. When all the carrot is in the jar, start to add more water until you have covered the carrot. There must be at least a 1in gap between the top of your water and the lid of your jar. This allows the fermenting magic some space to happen.

Leave the jar in a cool dark place for up to 2 weeks. You can taste it every few days to see how much ferment flavor you like. The longer you leave it, the sourer and more tangy it will become. When you are satisfied, pop the jar into the fridge and add to meals as you wish. This one is great with eggs and Mexican food.

cultured beets

Beetroot is one of my favorite foods to use as it holds so many health benefits. The thing about beetroot, and most foods, is that once you heat or cook the vegetable, it changes the medicinal properties. Many people cook up a big garlic based meal when they have a cold or flu, not realizing that heating the garlic will destroy many of its natural antimicrobial benefits. So, I am always looking for ways to enjoy the deep, earthy taste of raw beetroot. Culturing them is a great way to add softness whilst still maintaining, and in fact supercharging, the beetroot benefits.

INGREDIENTS

- 6-7 large organic beetroots
- 2 tablespoons wakame flakes (seaweed optional)
- 10 whole peppercorns
- 1-4 large chili (depending on how spicy you like it)
- 6 teaspoons of Himalayan salt
- 1 teaspoon food probiotics
- 4-5 cups of fresh filtered water, or enough to cover the beets
- Jar with clip lock lid and rubber seal

METHOD

Wash the beets and give them a scrub with a veggie scrubber do not peel. Cut the beets into pieces roughly about the size of a golf ball; they do not need to be perfect but try and get them around the same size as each other. Pop the cut beetroot into a large bowl. Put all the other ingredients in, except the water, and mix to coat the beetroot.

Put the beets into a large jar, pushing them down as you go. When all the mix is in the jar, start to add the water until you cover the lot. There must be at least a 1 inch gap between the top of the water and the lid of your jar. This allows the fermenting magic some space to happen.

Leave the jar in a cool dark place for up 4 weeks. Being a little bigger and harder than cabbage, the beets will take longer to ferment. You can taste it every few days, after the first 2 weeks, to see how much ferment flavor you like. The longer you leave it, the sourer and more tangy it will become. When you are satisfied, pop the jar into the fridge and add to meals as you wish. This one is great in salads or with antipasto.

kefir water

Kefir is a bacterial yeast culture that converts sugar into fructose and imparts incredible probiotic goodness into the water you keep it in. It is loaded with valuable enzymes, easily digestible sugars, beneficial acids, vitamins and minerals. It is a nice option if you are trying to avoid the caffeine present in kombucha, but still seeking a probiotic drink.

INGREDIENTS

- 100ml jar of water kefir grains
- 3 tablespoons organic raw sugar
- 1 tablespoon organic dried sultanas or apricots
- Pinch of bicarb & Himalayan salt
- 1l filtered water
- Jar with clip lock lid with rubber seal

METHOD

Mix the kefir grains, sugar, dried fruit, bicarb, and salt with the water in a 1 l click-lock jar. Leave to ferment for 12-48 hours. The higher the temperature where you leave the jar, the faster it will ferment.

By now it should be slightly fizzy and a bit sour and the sultanas should be dancing. Strain the water and keep the kefir grains aside for the next batch. Eat sultanas or apricots, or use in cooking. They are a great snack for kids. You can drink and enjoy your kefir as is or you can ferment again.

FLAVOURING IDEAS

- Honey & fresh grated ginger
- Passion fruit, peach, apple, berries, or mango (any fresh fruit really.)
- Use coconut water instead of water
- Experiment with different sugars such as molasses, coconut sugar and honey

kombucha

Kombucha has been around for centuries with cultures shared throughout communities. The major difference between it and kefir water is that kombucha uses tea and a SCOBY, while kefir uses water and grains. Unlike kefir, kombucha is aerobic, meaning it likes oxygen during its ferment. Both are full of vitamins, antioxidants, enzymes and good bacteria, so are great for our gut.

INGREDIENTS

- 1.5 l filtered water
- Organic black tea of your choice (3-6 bags or ¼ cup of loose tea leaves)
- ½ cup of organic sugar
- 1 healthy SCOBY
- 1 large jar, lid not needed

METHOD

To make kombucha you will need a SCOBY (Symbiotic Culture of Bacteria and Yeast). A SCOBY is a mushroom-like culture that will give your tea and water mixture all of its fermented goodness.

First make your sweet tea mix by brewing the tea in one litre of water for 5-6 minutes and strain. Add sugar and stir to dissolve. Put the tea into a large jar and top cup with the rest of water, set aside to cool. Once room temperature, add the SCOBY. Never put the SCOBY in hot water as it will die.

Cover the jar with a square of paper towel and place an elastic band around the outside to keep out any bugs. Put the jar in a corner of the kitchen where it won't be disturbed. Leave the kombucha to brew for at least 7 days. If it's your first batch, it can take cup to 14 days depending on the temperature at your home.

Start tasting it after 7 days. If it is too sweet then leave it longer. If it begins to taste too much like vinegar it has gone too long and you will need to rebrew for less time. The first batch will be the worst, it will only get better as your scoby strengthens and you gain confidence with fermenting.

Like kefir water, you can drink your kombucha after this first ferment. However, if you want to add a flavor, simply remove your scoby and store it in a seperate jar, immersed in half of the liquid. With the rest of the kombucha liquid add any fruit you desire into the jar and leave for 3 days. Once you have flavored your kombucha, remove the fruit and place in the fridge to stop the ferment process and enjoy at your leisure.

Start the process from the beginning again but when you add the scoby to this second batch also add the ½ cup of kombucha liquid reserved from your first ever batch. This will strengthen the brew and give a better flavor. Do this each time to continue the process and create a super kombucha.

FLAVOURING IDEAS

- Berries (fresh or frozen)
- Fresh lemon or lime juice
- A sliced apple
- Fresh watermelon and mint
- Or just keep it plain Jane!

pickling brine

Pickling food is an ancient way of preserving it, eradicating bad bacteria while isolating good bacteria and increasing bio-availability of the food. All of this adds to the health benefits of eating pickled food. The pickle itself will develop a different taste and texture to its fresh counterpart, adding to the diversity of your plate and palate. It is super easy to pickle most fruit and veg and you can play with the flavors by adding herbs and spices as well.

INGREDIENTS

- 1l filtered water
- ¼ cup apple cider vinegar
- 4 tablespoons of sugar
- 1 heaped teaspoon of salt

METHOD

Heat the water slightly and add the sugar. Stir until it has dissolved.
Add the vinegar and salt and mix well.
Use this as your pickling brine for the following pickles.

pickled jalapeños

Pickling is the easiest way to store vegetables and fruit for the future and it really is so easy. Before fridges were invented, everything was pickled, fermented or cured for preservation and longevity. These methods of food preparation also have the added benefit of preserving nutrients and in the case of fermenting, increasing the health benefits of the food. You can really pickle anything. Vegetables, fruits or meats. Here is my hubby's home pickled jalapeños. We grab them for anything from our Mexican feasts to a simple toasted sandwich for lunch. They live on our kitchen bench and get better with time. Try pickling carrot or ginger as well for added flavor to any meal.

INGREDIENTS

- 1kg jalapeños
- 1 small chili, sliced
- A pinch each of Himalayan salt & pepper
- 3 cloves of garlic, smashed
- White wine vinegar
- Jar with clip lock lid and rubber seal

METHOD

Grab your jalapeños and pierce the skin of each. Blanch in boiling water for 3 minutes. This will help them retain their texture.

Drain and pop aside to cool. Put the chili, salt, pepper and garlic in a large jar. Throw in all the jalapeños and fill to the top with vinegar and seal tight.

Leave for at least a week before trying. The longer you leave them, the stronger the heat and pickled flavor. The jar can be kept out of the fridge on the kitchen bench. Just grab one or two out when you want it.

The jalapeños will last forever as long as they are submerged.

quick cucumber pickle

We know fermented foods are good for us. But at home, I am also looking for something delicious to compliment a dish. This one adds texture, flavor and some kick-arse spice to the plate. It is refreshing, cooling and full of heat at the same time. It's even good on it's own- I often sneak a few pieces as I'm preparing the rest of the meal. Enjoy with any Japanese or Asian inspired dishes.

INGREDIENTS

- 2 medium cucumbers of your choice
- 4-5 tablespoons of white caramelized balsamic vinegar
- 2 tablespoons of gochugaru (large hot pepper available from asian grocers)
- ½ teaspoon salt

METHOD

Roughly slice cucumbers with the skin on into large diagonal chunks. Throw them into a large bowl with all the other ingredients and stir well to and coat.

Set them aside with a small plate covering the bowl for 10 minutes before serving. You can leave them longer if you wish. To store leftovers, just pop the cucumber into an airtight container for up to 1 week.

pickled carrots

Bright colored fruit and veg are loaded with antioxidants and healing nutrients that protect us from cancer and heart disease. Carrots in particular are the king of nutrition when it comes to root vegetables. They are packed with fibre, vitamin C and E and beta carotene. They help protect us against stroke, some cancers and lung disease, plus they help protect our sight.

INGREDIENTS

- 1kg carrots
- 700-900ml pickling brine
- 1l cliplock jar with rubber seal
- 3 tablespoons coriander seeds

METHOD

Slice carrot thinly with a mandolin or food processor. Pack the carrot tightly into the jar leaving a one inch gap from the top. Pour over the pickling brine so that all of the carrots are covered. Try and leave the small gap at the top as space for the vegetables to move. Pour in the coriander seeds and stir them around a little.

Clip the jar closed and set aside for 1-2 weeks before trying the carrot. You can leave pickles out of the fridge ongoing as they are now preserved. Just pull the pickles out as you want to eat them and seal the jar back up. Be sure to use clean tongs when getting pickles out.

These carrots are great on sandwiches and wraps, with Mexican food or with the supercharged koftas on page 209.

pickled red onion

Having onion raw is like having a supplement each day which may assist in protecting you from a range of bugs. Onion is anti-microbial and can help block carcinogens. They contain antioxidants that assist with nasal congestion so are perfect for a stuffy nose. Eating them pickled increases these compounds and also makes them more palatable than in their raw form. I am obsessed with adding pickled onion to my eggs in the morning.

INGREDIENTS

- 1kg red onion
- 700-900ml pickling brine
- 1l cliplock jar with rubber seal
- 3 tablespoons mustard seeds

METHOD

Slice the onion thinly with a mandolin or food processor. Pack the onion tightly into the jar leaving a one inch gap from the top. Pour over the pickling brine so that all onion is covered. Try and leave the small gap at the top as space for the vegetables to move. Pour in the mustard seeds and stir them around a little.

Clip the jar closed and set aside for 1-2 weeks before trying the onion. You can leave pickles out of the fridge ongoing as they are now preserved. Just pull the pickles out as you want to eat them and seal the jar back up. Be sure to use clean tongs when getting pickles out.

These onions are great on sandwiches, wraps, in curries like a butter chicken (page 214) and especially with the roast lamb with cumin and lemon (page 210).

japanese ginger pickle

INGREDIENTS

- 500g fresh ginger
- 750ml clip lock jar with rubber seal
- 500ml pickling brine
- 1 teaspoon extra sugar

OPTIONAL SPICE

- 2 tablespoons gochugaru
- 3 fresh chili's

METHOD

Peel the ginger as best you can. Don't worry if there is a bit of skin here and there. Slice the ginger thinly with a mandolin or food processor. Pack the ginger tightly into the jar leaving a one inch gap from the top. Add extra sugar to the brine and pour pickling brine over ginger until it is covered. Try and leave the small gap at the top as space for the vegetables to move. Pour in the chili if you want spicy ginger and stir them around a little.

Clip the jar closed and set aside for 1-2 weeks before trying the ginger. You can leave pickles out of the fridge ongoing as they are now preserved. Just pull the pickles out as you want to eat them and seal the jar back up. Be sure to use clean tongs when getting pickles out.

quick pickled mushrooms

INGREDIENTS

- 1 tablespoon olive oil
- 4 garlic cloves, smashed with the back of the knife
- 100g of mixed mushrooms
- 2 sprigs of thyme
- 1 small chili, roughly chopped
- 4 tablespoons of white wine or apple cider vinegar
- 2 anchovies
- Fresh cracked pepper

METHOD

Pop olive oil and garlic into a frypan on medium heat until soft and lightly browned. Add mushrooms and cook for 2 minutes, stirring. Add all other ingredients and simmer on low for around 10 minutes stirring constantly, until mushrooms are soft and cooked through.

Eat warm as is or pop into a jar and store in the fridge for up to 2 weeks. These mushrooms are perfect to enlighten a simple fried egg or add punch to any vegetarian meal.

pickled garlic

INGREDIENTS

- 10-20 whole garlic bulbs
- 1l cliplock jar with rubber seal
- 700-900ml pickling brine

METHOD

Pack the garlic bulbs tightly into the jar leaving a one inch gap from the top. Pour over the pickling brine so that all garlic is covered. Try and leave the small gap at the top as space for the vegetables to move.

Clip the jar closed and set aside for 3 weeks before eating the first of the garlic. You can leave pickles out of the fridge ongoing as they are now preserved. Just pull the pickles out as you want to eat them and seal the jar back up. Be sure to use clean tongs when getting pickles out.

This garlic is perfect for using in any Asian inspired meals including jazzing up a mid-week stir fry.

Chapter 2
BRAISING, BOILING & BROTHING

Just like fermenting, slow cooking allows the food to be broken down and release all of its goodness. This makes it a hell of a lot easier for your gut to absorb the nutrients and allows you to get the most out of all the beautiful foods you are eating. These meals are easy on a tired gut and will give it time to heal while still feeding and nurturing it. They are also perfect for chronically ill people who find it difficult to break down food, as well as children and the elderly.

Why do we eat chicken soup or comforting broths when we are sick? Because they are easy to digest and give our body nutrition whilst not taking any energy away from the healing process. I love to put split shin bones from my local meat man under the grill with a little salt and pepper for 15 minutes or so and then devour the inside marrow. It is sweet and succulent and so nutritious. Bones are not just one of my favorite things to eat, but if you have watched My Kitchen Rules or MasterChef lately you will have noticed there is a lot of bone marrow being used and fed to the judges. This is a sure-fire way to impress them and get a good score. Chefs have appreciated the value, flavor and taste of bone marrow, knowing it is irreplaceable in cooking far longer than most have been turning their noses up at it. If you have ever had a good quality jus at a restaurant you would have likely enjoyed the complexity and depth that bone marrow has given to that sauce in its infancy. Or if you are like me, you may just like to go straight to the source and grill a bone.

Bones are full of collagen, gelatin, amino acids and minerals in a form that is easy for your body to absorb including calcium, magnesium, glucosamine and silicon. Using bones will assist in bringing the junctions of the gut tightly together, treating leaky gut syndrome. Many of my clients have found that after drinking bone broths they have overcome food intolerances and allergies have dissipated. Bones are also the perfect anti-aging medicine, great for joint health, reducing inflammation and cellulite, plus boosting the immune system.

RESPONSIBLE MEATING

I love to eat and I love to eat meat. My husband and I fell in love over our first breakfast together where I surprised him by ordering the exact same as he had. Bacon, eggs, chevapi, tomatoes, avocado, spinach, tomato and roast pumpkin. Although we both love meat we are picky about the quality of our meat and have grown together in an ethical approach to the meat we choose.

Eating animals ethically for us means that we have adopted the philosophy of eating snout to tail. Learning what the animal has eaten itself and finding animals that have had happy lives and have been slaughtered ethically is of the upmost importance. This means that we can feed ourselves on an entire animal, rather than selected parts. We believe that by eating parts of the animal that others do not, less animals will need to be slaughtered.

My hope is that I can teach others how to do this, so that everyone is not buying chicken breast and thigh alone while the rest of the chicken is cast aside. By cooking a whole chicken and creating a beautifully balanced meal with ample sides we can feed a whole family of four. When we use chicken breast alone we need to kill two chickens to get a breast each and feed that same family. Plus, all of the natural fat from that chicken has been sliced away so we need more food to keep us full and satisfied. Do a simple test at home by trying both chicken dinners and see which one feeds your family better, leaves them feeling full and negates the need for after dinner snacks.

Another big part of our journey has involved the way we eat at home and share our food. There is so much joy in sharing food and engaging with food. By cooking a whole chicken, we engage with the fact that it is a chicken. We can be grateful for its sustenance, but most of all we can place it in the middle of the table, surrounded by salad or veg and we can share it.

I have learned over time that most cultures with rich culinary history eat this way, by placing all the food down in the middle of the table and passing it around. By dishing up the meal for each family member we not only take away autonomy over food, we also often over feed ourselves. By

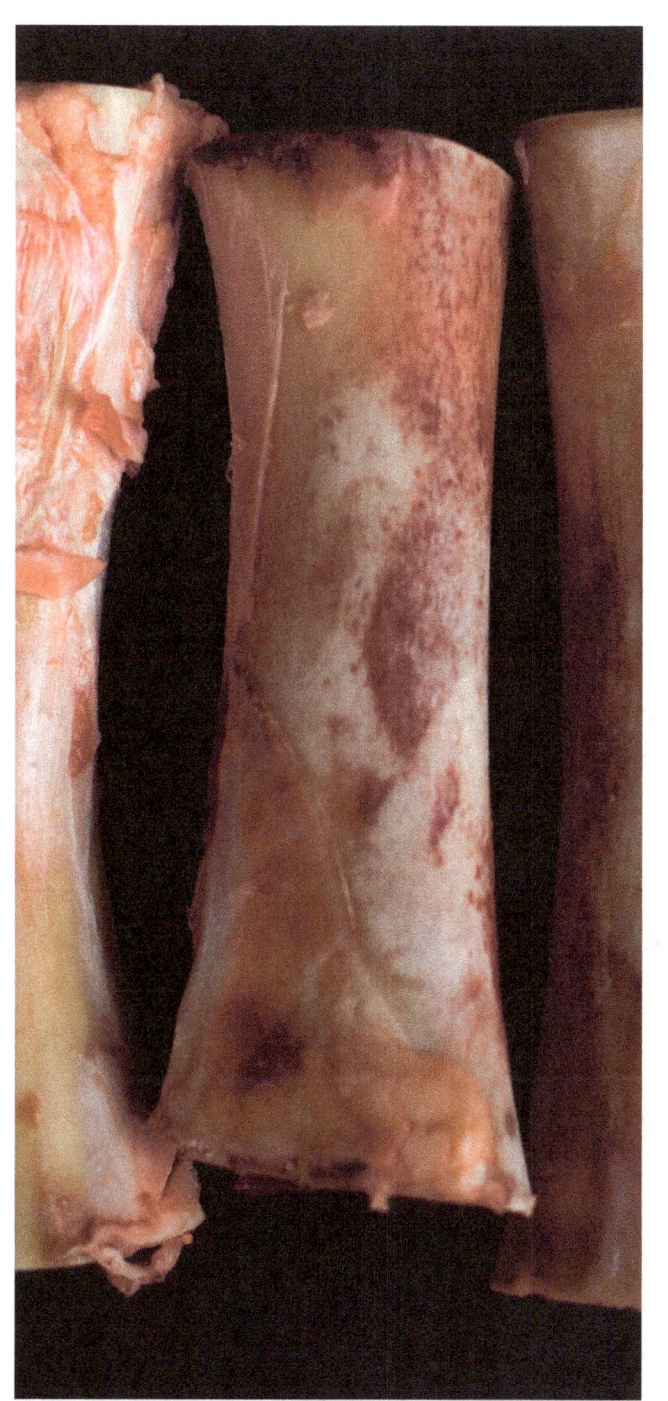

placing the food on the table, we are less likely to over eat and are more likely to engage with both our food and those we are sharing it with.

For children, autonomy over food is extremely important. Often food and what is actually put into the mouth is the single thing that they have control over, so it is important to nourish this as much as possible. I can imagine that many parents reading this are thinking that if they put the food out on the table and do not serve portions, that the child will simply chose not to eat the broccoli and peas, stocking up on mashed potato instead. I have found this is not the case. Kids are much more likely to choose new foods of their own accord, plus serving themselves is exciting and fun. You may also like to try some simple rules around getting something from each bowl on the table to put on their own plate or trying a certain number of different things each night.

WHY COOK SLOWLY?

Just like fermenting, slow cooking allows the food to be broken down and release all of its goodness. This makes it a hell of a lot easier for your gut to absorb the nutrients and allow you to get the most out of all the beautiful foods you are eating.

These meals are easy on a tired gut and will give it time to heal while still feeding and nurturing it. They are also perfect for chronically ill people who find it difficult to break down food, as well as children and the elderly.

Why do we eat chicken soup or comforting broths when we are sick? Because they are easy to digest and give our body nutrition whilst not taking any energy away from the healing process. I love to put split shin bones from my local meat man under the grill with a little salt and pepper for 15 minutes or so and then devour the inside marrow. It is sweet and succulent and so nutritious. Bones are not just one of my favorite things to eat, but if you have watched My Kitchen Rules or MasterChef lately you will have noticed there is a lot of bone marrow being used and fed to the judges. This is a sure-fire way to impress them and get a good score. Chefs have appreciated the value, flavor and taste of bone marrow, knowing it is irreplaceable in cooking far longer than most have been turning their noses cup at it. If you have ever had a good quality jus at a restaurant you would have likely enjoyed the complexity and depth that bone marrow has given to that sauce in its infancy. Or if you are like me, you may just like to go straight to the source and grill a bone.

Bones are full of collagen, gelatin, amino acids and minerals in a form that is easy for your body to absorb including calcium, magnesium, glucosamine and silicon. Using bones will assist in bringing the junctions of the gut tightly together, treating leaky gut syndrome. Many of my clients have found that after drinking bone broths they have overcome food intolerances and allergies have dissipated. Bones are also the perfect anti-aging medicine, great for joint health, reducing inflammation and cellulite, plus boosting the immune system.

DOS & DON'TS OF BROTHING

DO:

1. Use grass fed bones
2. Use organic or pesticide free vegetables
3. Use filtered water
4. Roast your bones for a stronger beef flavor
5. Pop a lid on so your broth doesn't evaporate
6. Use a slow cooker or pressure cooker

DON'T:

1. Use a pot that is too small
2. Take it off too early
3. Let it cool slowly—strain, cool and refrigerate as soon as possible
4. Leave all the goodness inside your bones—get that marrow out before discarding the bones and add to your broth
5. Think you are wasting the veggies—all of the nutrition has been transferred into your broth

bone broth

Broth is enormously healing, filling, and nutritious. Enjoy it every day for breakfast or lunch if you wish! When it comes to your bones, grass-fed is more important than organic. Buy good quality beef bones from the butcher. You can roast off beef bones with olive oil, salt, and pepper for 10-15 minutes before putting them in the pot for a stronger flavored broth.

INGREDIENTS

- 6 good quality bones (I use split shin bones for a more gelatinous broth)
- 1 tablespoon apple cider vinegar
- 3 generous pinches salt
- Lots of fresh cracked pepper
- Fresh corn cob, husk removed
- 2-3 carrots, sliced (unpeeled)
- 1 bulb of garlic, chopped in half through the cloves (skin and all)
- 1 bunch of parsley, include stems
- Leftover kale stalks
- 2 sticks of celery halved, or enough to fit in pot (including leaves)
- Fresh filtered water to cover the above

METHOD

Throw all the ingredients into a stock pot or large saucepan. Put on low to medium heat to simmer, covered with the lid, for 4-12 hours. The longer you leave the broth simmering, the more nutrients you will receive. I do mine for at least 8 hours.

Once cooled, strain all veggies and bones out (save liquid).

Store your broth in air tight glass containers in the fridge after it's cooled. It will last up to one week in the fridge, and up to 6 months in the freezer. Freeze in small batches for easy thawing, or even in ice cube trays for when recipes call for stock.

Season to taste and add other goodies into the broth when you're ready to eat.

chicken broth

Use in soups, stews, casseroles, spaghetti and rice dishes and to replace all store-bought stock cubes and powder. Even add a little to scrambled eggs for a flavor burst and as extra gut gold.

INGREDIENTS

- 1 good quality chicken frame (organic, free range if possible)
- 3 carrots, chopped roughly (unpeeled)
- 1 onion, cut in half (skin and all)
- 1 bulb of garlic, chopped in half through the cloves (skin and all)
- 3 stalks of celery, broken in half or enough to fit in pot (include leaves)
- 1 punch of parsley, including stems
- Salt and pepper to taste
- Fresh filtered water to cover the above

METHOD

Put all of your ingredients in a large pot on a medium to low heat, and cover with water.

Pop the lid on once your heat is steady and it is not going to bubble over. Let it simmer away for 4 hours or more. Chicken broth does not need as long as beef as the bones are not as hard and big.

Strain and discard chicken frame and veggies. Store in airtight glass jars in the fridge and/or freezer.

broth brekkie

This is such a great way to eat in the morning. In Japan, a simple broth with some leftover meat and whatever veggies are in the house is always on the breakfast menu. For some, moving away from cereals is difficult and trying what is normally considered lunch or dinner foods first thing can be a challenge. However, if you create a simple meal you love you will soon adjust, plus you will reap all the benefits of a fully balanced start to the day rather than the sugar spike that cereal and muesli can create.

INGREDIENTS

- 1 cup of homemade broth (chicken or beef)
- 1 slice of brisket (or any other meat you have leftover)
- A few ribbons of carrot and zucchini
- A couple of broccoli florets, or any of your other fav veggies

METHOD

Heat the broth in a small saucepan for 5 minutes.
Throw in the piece of brisket for a few minutes to heat through.
Transfer to a bowl, add your veg and enjoy.

This is perfect on a cold winter morning to get you warmed up and ready for the day.

a morning brothee

This brothee can easily replace a morning coffee and will serve as a beautiful breakfast as it is so filling and nutritious. My hubby loves it with a big slosh of Tabasco hot sauce to get his morning started. If you are new to broths and have had a low-fat diet in the past just keep in mind that this will be very filling. Start small and drink it slow until you adjust. You can see the melted coconut oil floating on top waiting to be gobbled up.

INGREDIENTS

- 1 cup of homemade broth (beef or chicken)
- 1 tablespoon of coconut oil
- 1 teaspoon grass-fed butter
- A pinch of cumin and cayenne (optional)
- Salt and pepper to taste

METHOD

Heat up the broth and pour into a big coffee mug.

Put oil, butter and spices in. Season to taste and drink slowly while you get yourself ready for your day.

short ribs

Beef short ribs are easy and filling. They are classic comfort food and are perfect for a cold winter night—though we tend to have them all year round. They are also great the next day for lunch in a salad or on a wrap.

INGREDIENTS

- 2 kg beef short ribs, on the bone
- 2 cans of diced tomatoes
- 4 fresh tomatoes, quartered
- 1 cup preservative free red wine
- 1 cup bone broth
- 1 handful of fresh thyme
- 1 handful of fresh oregano
- ½ teaspoon salt
- Freshly cracked pepper

METHOD

Throw all ingredients into a large casserole dish with a lid. Mix it up so all the beef is coated. The liquid should almost cover all the meat- about ¾ of the way up.

Place the lid on and pop into the oven at 180°C for as long as you have to spare. It needs a minimum of 4 hours to work its magic but 6 hours makes a delicious and extremely tender dish.

Enjoy with sweet tatie mash (page 121) and steamed greens.

pressure pork belly

Who can resist? Braising in this way will bring out the best in the meat making it succulent and juicy. And with a pressure cooker you can skip the hours of cooking in messy fat. This pork belly takes only 30 minutes from start to finish giving you just enough time to prep some sides ready for when it comes out.

INGREDIENTS

- 1 kg pork belly
- 1 cup tamari, soy sauce or Braggs aminos
- ½ cup bone broth-or just enough to cover pork
- 3 small fresh chilis
- 1 tablespoon apple cider vinegar
- 6 cloves of garlic, whole, smashed (can leave skin on)
- 3 star anise, whole
- Extra chili flakes to taste

METHOD

Add all ingredients into the pressure cooker and stir a little.
Set on PRESSURE COOK, MEAT, for 30 minutes.

Ensure pork is cooked by placing a fork through it. It should be soft and juicy and easy to tear apart. If not, give it another 10 minutes.

Enjoy with rice and fresh steamed greens.

brisket

Brisket is a traditional Jewish meat and also became popular for smoking in Texas. Although it is now a sought-after cut of meat and most love to eat it once they have tried it, brisket originated for the same reason most of the recipes in this book have-because it was cheap. There is a rich history in cooking brisket and every brisket recipe is different but one thing never changes. The slower you cook it the more succulent the meat will be. Many of these meats were cheap because they take a long time to cook, like lamb shanks, but are now popular and can be quite expensive. My Nan flat out refuses to pay such a premium for shanks now as they used to be basically thrown away when she raised my Dad and it was something they ate often because of its low cost. Smoking brisket is an art form of its own but that's not what I have given you as I do not have a smoker-but boy if I had the space for one. This is my take on an easy way to prep and cook brisket and you will be surprised how filling it is and how long it feeds the family for. It is perfect for sandwiches the next day or try it in some broth for breakfast.

INGREDIENTS

- 1kg good quality cut of brisket, fat on
- Olive oil to coat, about 6 tablespoons
- Spices of your choice-I like to use cumin, paprika and cayenne
- Salt and pepper to taste
- 1 medium sweet potato, roughly chopped
- 6 organic potatoes, washed (unpeeled)
- 3 carrots, broken in half
- 2 lemons halved, juices squeezed over meat and thrown in
- 2 onions, halved with skin on
- 2 cups of your homemade stock

METHOD

Put the brisket fat side up in a large, deep, heavy based baking tray. Rub it down with oil, spices, salt and pepper.

Throw all the veg, including the squeezed lemon halves, into the tray, placing them under the brisket so it lifts it off the bottom of the tray. Add enough homemade stock (broth) to touch the underside of the brisket but not cover it.

Cover with a lid or aluminium foil (be sure the foil is not touching your meat) and place in the oven at 150°C, for about 6 hours or until the meat pulls away without force.

beef cheek stew

You will need a slow cooker or pressure cooker for this recipe. This way you can put it on and leave it to work its magic. If you don't have one I suggest you invest in one as they make meal prep a whole lot easier but if not then just use your oven and a deep casserole dish. The slower and lower you can cook cheeks the better.

INGREDIENTS

- 1kg beef cheeks
- 2-6 tablespoons olive oil
- 2 large onions, cut roughly
- 4-6 cloves of garlic
- 2 carrots, chopped roughly
- The rind of half an orange, cut into thin strips
- Juice of 1 whole orange
- ½ cup homemade beef broth
- ½ cup red wine (optional) or use water
- 2 large handfuls of pitted olives of your choice

METHOD

Brown the beef cheeks using the olive oil. Use a fry pan or your pressure cooker for this on a high heat. Set them aside once browned. The caramelization on the cheeks is key to getting a strong flavor through your stew so don't rush this part or crowd the pan and it will be worth the effort. Use a little more oil to soften the onions and garlic. You want them to become translucent and soft, not browned so keep the temp low here and give them a few more minutes than you normally would. Again, this will add to the depth of flavor.

Throw in the carrots and give them 5 minutes before adding beef cheeks and any juice back into the cooker, or transferring all ingredients to the slow cooker or oven tray. Add in orange rind, juice, broth and wine. Ensure there is enough liquid to cover all the cheeks but don't flood them (especially if using water) as this will dilute the flavor. Put the pressure cooker on MEAT and PRESSURE for 1 hour.

Check after the hour and see if the beef cheeks are beginning to fall apart. They will likely need another 45 minutes on the same setting. Once they are soft as butter, remove the cheeks and put the cooker on high again to start reducing the sauce. This will take around 15 minutes, stirring as needed. If you are using a slow cooker, set it on low and leave it for 4-6 hours. Once the cheeks are cooked, remove them and pour the liquid into a saucepan to reduce. If you are using the oven, you will need to give the cheeks 6-8 hours on 165°C. Check them every few hours, ensuring the liquid doesn't dry up. Once they're falling apart remove them and pour the liquid into a saucepan to reduce.

When ready to dish up, put everything back in the pot, add the olives, and serve hot with sweet tatie mash (page 121) and greens.

asian poached chicken

Using a whole chicken will give a much better yield than single parts. This means it will feed the family better and works out cheaper. We are also then harnessing the power of the entire animal and all it has to offer. This recipe gives you a beautiful broth to enjoy with it or to save and use as stock. I like to shred the chicken, serve with a crunchy cabbage salad and have the broth in a little cup on the side.

INGREDIENTS

- 1 whole chicken, rinsed
- 2l filtered water (or enough to cover the chicken)
- 1 bunch of coriander, chopped
- 2-3 sticks of fresh lemongrass
- 6 cloves
- 1 bulb of garlic, slice in half lengthways
- 6 spring onion stalks, chopped roughly
- 1 large piece of ginger, skinned and chopped roughly
- 2-3 chili's, sliced lengthways (optional)
- 4 tablespoons soy sauce
- 2 tablespoons fish sauce

METHOD

Place the chicken in a deep, thick bottomed casserole dish or saucepan. Since the chicken will be cooking in the broth for some time the thick base will help prevent burning. Add all other ingredients and bring to a soft boil.

Turn down the heat to low, cover and leave for 45 minutes.

At this point check the chicken by sliding a knife between the leg and body and checking if the meat is cooked. It may take an hour or so depending on the size of your chicken and the temperature. If the leg comes away and the meat is white, take the chicken out. If it needs a little longer keep an eye on it so it doesn't overcook.

Remove the chicken and set aside.

Turn the heat up to a simmer and keep the lid off to reduce the broth for 10-20 minutes. I like a strong broth so I leave it a little longer. Just keep tasting it and turn it off once it reaches the desired flavor.

Strain the broth before serving. This delicious, easy to digest and gut healing broth will keep in the fridge for a week or freeze for up to 3 months.

orange, thyme & fig pressure cooked chicken

INGREDIENTS

- 1 whole chicken, rinsed with filtered water
- 4 large cubes of salted butter
- 5 sprigs of fresh thyme
- ½ cup fresh parsley, roughly chopped
- 1 orange
- 5 whole figs
- 1 cup verjuice (or broth)
- Salt and pepper to season

METHOD

Stuff the chicken with the butter, thyme and parsley. Place the chicken into the pressure cooker pot. Slice the orange and give each a squeeze over the chicken before dropping them in skin and all. Add the figs and verjuice to the pot and season with salt and pepper over the top. Keep in mind the butter is salted, so you will not need as much as usual.

Put the lid on the pressure cooker and set to MEAT for 30 minutes. Once the pressure cooker is finished release the steam and check the chicken is cooked by pulling one of the legs away from the body and ensuring the juices run clear.

Enjoy the chicken pulled over a fresh salad or with loads of beautiful steamed vegetables.

Chapter 3
OFFAL—IS NOT AWFUL

Offal is not awful. These parts of animals were traditionally the parts fought over at the family dinner table as they were so tasty. In many cultures, the brain is the most prized part of the animal. It is so delicious that it is hidden from children for the adults to enjoy alone. Organ meats are also more nutritious than the lean muscle counterparts.

It is so interesting to me that our 'normal' food choices, including what cuts of meat we eat, are culturally determined. As an adult, it is not difficult for me to try new parts of animals as I had some experience growing up with offal, but it can be overwhelming for those who are new to it. Start slow and introduce small amounts of offal into the normal foods that you enjoy at home.

If you have had a bad offal experience than you just haven't tried it in the right way. Make it how you feel you would like it. If you are just starting out, don't go for the full offal. Start by adding it to your normal weekly meals. Make a pie with some kidney cut through it. Add some liver to your spaghetti bowl. Don't overdo it—just a little each week will add buckets of nutrients.

The most important thing about offal is the quality. We need to ensure that the offal we are eating is from an animal that has been cared for, loved and fed well. Grass fed, not grain fed.

Eating the whole animal

I am a huge believer in eating the whole animal. We cannot continue to eat selective parts of animals. If we wish to consume animals in a sustainable, respectful and traditional way, we must adopt a top to tail mentality and begin to eat and utilise as much of that animal as possible. Otherwise, it's sacrifice was in vain and we are truly crushing the world with our footprint.

grandad's lamb fry

My Grandad rarely left the house without a hot breakfast. He was often in the kitchen and I much preferred his cooking to my Grandmas. I would sleep over in pure anticipation for breakfast, whatever it might be, and would wake early before he left for work to eat with him. To me, any hot breakfast is still the best kind of breakfast. He would cook this lamb fry but we were both just as happy with a steak stew from a tin can. My love of morning meat has never diminished but I find myself choosing this over the canned steak these days.

INGREDIENTS

- 1 tablespoon butter
- ½ onion, chopped roughly
- 1 clove garlic, smashed
- 2 tomatoes, chopped roughly
- 5-6 button mushrooms, cut in half
- 250g lamb liver, chopped into bite sized pieces
- 1 zucchini, chopped into bite sized pieces
- 3 tablespoons bone or chicken broth
- ½ teaspoon cayenne pepper (optional)
- Salt and pepper to taste
- A handful of English spinach, washed
- Juice of ½ fresh lemon, to serve
- 1 teaspoon pepita seeds, to serve

METHOD

Pop the butter in a heavy based saucepan over medium heat, and add in onion and garlic. Cook for 5-10 minutes until translucent and soft. Add tomatoes and stir through for about 5 minutes until starting to breakdown.

Throw in the mushrooms for another 5 minutes, stirring to combine. Add the liver and cook until nearly all browned and then throw in zucchini pieces for another 5 minutes, allowing them to get some color. Add in the broth, cayenne, and salt and pepper. Stir together well.

Put some English spinach in the bottom of a bowl and top with hot lamb's fry. Squeeze fresh lemon over the top and sprinkle some pepitas over as well.

Enjoy this fresh take on an old favorite.

cold tripe salad

I know you are probably thinking that the only thing worse than tripe could be cold tripe, but don't knock it until you try it. This is my take on Fuqi Feipian, a traditional, very spicy, Chinese-style tripe salad which is still a popular dish today. It is super yummy topped with cashews for a little extra crunch, and a refreshing side salad of crisp cabbage and lettuce.

INGREDIENTS

- 1 tablespoon olive oil
- 1 large red onion, sliced thinly
- 1 garlic clove, diced
- 2 cm piece fresh ginger, peeled and sliced thinly
- 3 large red chilies, sliced with seeds
- ¼ cup red wine vinegar
- 2 tablespoons fermented soy sauce
- 300g tripe, washed and cut into 1-2cm pieces
- 300g beef eye fillet, cut into thin strips
- 1 can of organic black beans, rinsed and drained
- 1 teaspoon sesame oil
- 1 teaspoon sesame seeds
- ½ bunch fresh coriander, chopped roughly, include stalks

METHOD

Heat oil in a large heavy based fry pan and cook off onion, garlic, ginger and chili for 5 minutes or until soft. Add vinegar and soy and bring to a boil. Add the tripe and cook for about 15 minutes or until soft. Transfer to a bowl and allow to cool.

Put the fry pan back on the heat and get it hot. Throw the pieces of steak in and cook for 2-3 minutes, leaving them soft and as rare as possible. Transfer to the tripe bowl and allow to cool.

Once cooled, put the rest of the ingredients into the large bowl and mix.

Garnish with fresh chili and coriander to serve.

warm tripe stew

I understand if you can't come at cold tripe salad, so here is a warm dish for you to try. This recipe is my version of a traditional Italian favorite with succulent, melt in the mouth tripe and a homestyle tomato sauce.

INGREDIENTS

- 1 kg honeycomb tripe
- 1 tablespoon apple cider vinegar
- 1 teaspoon honey
- 2 tablespoons olive oil
- 2 large red onions, roughly chopped
- 6 cloves of garlic, smashed
- 2 large carrots, diced
- 2 cans of whole tomatoes
- handful of fresh oregano, chopped roughly
- handful of fresh parsley, chopped roughly
- 1 cup bone broth
- 1 cup of preservative free red wine
- 2 teaspoons salt

METHOD

Place the tripe in a large saucepan and cover with filtered water. Add apple cider vinegar and honey and bring to boil. Reduce to simmer, cover and leave for around 2 hours or until soft and tender. Drain and set aside.

Add olive oil into a large saucepan and throw in onions, garlic and carrots. Cook for 2-3 minutes until starting to soften. Add canned tomatoes, fresh herbs, bone broth, wine and salt and stir bringing to a strong simmer. Allow the sauce to cook off for around 20 minutes.

In the meantime, slice the tripe into large pieces. Once the sauce has thickened add the tripe and stir. Turn the heat down and leave for 10 minutes to heat through.

Serve hot with fresh parsley and a squeeze of lemon.

homemade pâté

Chicken livers are chock full of protein, folate, vitamin A, C, D, and zinc. These are some of the essential nutrients for our immune system and therefore our gut. Liver really is a meat multi-vitamin, plus is less expensive and easier to absorb than the ones off the shelf. As the liver is an excretory organ in all animals we need to be mindful of the quality of liver we buy and eat. Go for grass-fed and/or organic liver where possible to reduce your exposure to antibiotics, hormones, herbicides and pesticides. Look for bright red liver which still has a perfusion of blood vessels. This is a good indication that it is fresh and many of the nutrients we are aiming to get are in that blood, including CoQ10. Liver is one of the few offal that is enjoyed in some cultures raw. While we don't need to eat it every day, liver in small amounts can serve as a fantastic additional to your diet.

INGREDIENTS

- 500g of organic chicken livers
- 1 clove of garlic, crushed
- ½ cup of butter (or ghee or coconut oil)
- 1 pinch of salt
- Lots of freshly cracked black pepper (to taste)
- 1 tablespoon olive oil
- Juice of ½ an orange
- The delicate leaves from 4 sprigs of thyme

METHOD

Cook the chicken livers and garlic in fry pan in batches over medium heat and set aside. Don't overcook. They only need few minutes on each side. Set aside livers and pop the butter into the pan until just melted do not boil.

Place livers into a blender, food processor, or use a small stick blender to start to break them down. Add the melted butter slowly to the livers while processing.

When you have a smooth paste, add all other ingredients and stir with a wooden spoon. Pack the mixture into a jam jar and place into the fridge to set.

Pâté is amazing for breakfast. Try on some toast with fresh cut tomato and a pinch more salt on top.

lamb brains

Every other week my grandad would take me to the local club for lambs brains. After many trips, I asked him what they actually were. He replied that they were lambs brains (of course) in his matter of fact country style. Unsure and slightly confused I asked again. I knew that they were called lambs brains but what were they really made of? The brain of a lamb, he explained. I was disgusted. I couldn't believe that he had been feeding me real brains all this time. I told my parents as soon as we got home and they laughed, but my Dad explained that it was just like any other meat that I ate. It all came from an animal and at the time lamb cutlets were one of my favorite dinners, so the brains I had been eating were from the same animal. This helped immensely as my own little brain ticked over. I was however so upset with Grandad that I didn't go to the club for a whole month before I missed it and forgave him.

INGREDIENTS

- ½ cup coconut oil
- 6 juicy lamb brains
- 2 beaten eggs
- ½ cup of organic gluten free flour or rice or potato (try spelt if you are not gluten free)
- ½ teaspoon smoked paprika
- Good pinch of salt and pepper
- Optional – small handful of parmesan cheese or dairy/soy free cheese such as Daiya (available from health food shops)
- 1 fresh lemon, sliced
- A handful of roughly chopped fresh parsley

METHOD

Put the coconut oil into a heavy based fry pan on a medium-high heat.

Throw the lambs brains into the egg mixture and let them sit. In a separate bowl mix all other ingredients- leaving the lemon and parsley aside for serving. Grab a brain and make sure it is coated well with egg and then coat it in the flour mixture and throw it into the pan. Give them plenty of room and don't overcrowd the pan. They will take about 2 minutes each side or until golden. Place on paper towel to rest. You may need to throw in some fresh oil as you go. Complete the same steps in small batches, and place on towel with others.

Serve with freshly squeezed lemon and fresh parsley, and a little homemade mayo if you like. These brains are also great with the lemon and fennel salad (page 138) or try it the club way with baked veggies and greens, just like when I was a kid.

black breakfast

This is an easy way to start introducing new flavors to your palate and the families. Black pudding has actually been termed a superfood due to its high protein content. It is also full of iron, zinc and good fat. It is really important to grab a good quality sausage so that it is fresh and not highly processed, full of cooking salt and preservatives. You can usually get this from a goodquality butcher. Remember, our brain is 60% fat, so we need to feed it with good fats every day.

INGREDIENTS

- 1 tomato, halved
- ½ cup mushrooms, halved
- ½ avocado
- 1-2 eggs
- 1-2 black pudding sausages, sliced at an angle

METHOD

Simply fry up your favorite Sunday morning breakfast. Eggs, tomato, mushies and avocado work well. Grill some tomatoes and sauté some mushies with a bit of coconut oil, salt and pepper for a yummy side.

While the eggs are cooking (however you like), slice off some black pudding and throw it in the pan. It only needs a few minutes on each side to caramelize and heat through.

Put it all on a plate with a side of sliced avocado and dig into this protein-filled brekkie.

The best part is that you can do it all in the one frypan. Let's move away from toast and high-carb cereals and back to a real and nourishing breakfast.

nana's steak & kidney pie

I love a good pie to come home to so I tend to prep the filling the day before. Then when I get home from work I can throw the pastry on top, pop it in the oven and it's ready in no time. This is such a classic, nourishing winter meal.

INGREDIENTS

For the pie filling:
- Butter and olive oil for frying
- 2 onions, chopped roughly
- 2 carrots, diced
- 2 celery stalks, diced
- 4 cloves of garlic, smashed
- 1 kg chuck steak, cut into chunks
- 200g lamb kidneys, cut into chunks
- 2 tablespoons gluten free flour to thicken
- 2 cups homemade beef broth
- 1 can whole tomatoes
- 3 handfuls of mushrooms (I like to use Swiss but any will work)
- 3 bay leaves
- 1 teaspoon chili flakes (optional)
- 6 stalks of parsley, stems & leaves, chopped roughly
- 4 sprigs of thyme, whole

For the flakey pastry:
- 2 cups flour (you can use spelt, wheat, or gluten free plain flour)
- Pinch of salt
- ½ cup unsalted butter, cold, cut into cubes
- 1 egg
- Up to ¾ cup water start slow as you may not need it all
- Extra flour for dusting and rolling

METHOD

Preheat oven to 170°C. On a medium heat in a deep-set casserole dish (that has a lid for later) fry onion, carrot, celery and garlic until soft and translucent. This is the base of flavor that will build your filling so take your time. Make sure there is plenty of melted butter and oil in there while frying. Take out and set aside.

Turn up the heat and add steak, tossing until brown. Set aside and do the same with kidneys. Don't overcook the kidneys. They will only take about 5 minutes to brown. Add veg and steak back into the dish with the kidneys. Add flour and cook off for 3-4 minutes or until all fat is soaked up and bottom of the pan is dry and sticking.

Add wine and scrape all the sticky goodness from the pan (deglaze) and allow to cook off alcohol for 2 minutes. Add broth, tomatoes, mushrooms, herbs and spices and mix well. Pop the lid on and place in the oven for 2 hours. Stir a few times during this time. Remove lid for the last half hour to allow mix to thicken. Check to make sure there is plenty of liquid left. Give it a stir or two before popping it back into the oven for the remaining 30 minutes.

When you're ready to cook and eat, then it's time to make the pastry. I find it super easy to pop all this in the food processor. Throw in flour, salt and butter first and process until crumbly. Add egg and give it a buzz. Start to add water and process in single buzzes until the mix suddenly balls together. Stop adding water and pop it onto a floured surface.

Knead the dough to bring it together and then roll out with a rolling pin. Don't worry if it breaks apart a little you can fix it once it's on the pie. Place the dough on top of the pie and pop it in the oven on 180°C, for around 20 minutes or until crust is golden.

beef & heart pie

This pie is easy on the weeknights as it has what my husband calls a "fake roof". No need to make pastry, easy to prepare in advance and throw in the oven when you get home! It's also an easy and sneaky way to get the nutrient-dense heart into the kids, and even for some of us adults who are a bit unsure. Heart has a higher protein content than steak and is full of B vitamins, antioxidants, zinc and CQ10. It's cheap, filling and super healthy. This one is easiest in the pressure cooker. If you don't have one, use your slow cooker for the first part and a saucepan to reduce the gravy. It will take around 4 hours in the slow cooker and 45 mins in a pressure cooker. Well worth the investment in a pressure cooker, I say!

INGREDIENTS

For the pie filling:
- 500g chuck or oyster steak
- 250g ox or beef heart
- 2 tablespoons olive oil
- 2 red onions, peeled & sliced thickly
- 3 garlic cloves
- 1 carrot, roughly diced
- 1 can whole tomatoes
- ½ cup peas
- 1 cup red wine
- 1 cup broth or stock
- 1 teaspoon mustard seeds
- 2 teaspoons dried oregano
- 1 teaspoon salt
- Fresh cracked pepper to taste

For the fake roof:
- 2 medium sweet potatoes
- 3 white potatoes
- 3-4 tablespoons butter

METHOD

Chop the steak and heart roughly into medium bite sized pieces and throw into the pressure cooker with the olive oil. Set to HIGH heat SAUTE. If using a slow cooker do this in a frying pan on medium to high heat first. Throw in the onions and garlic and allow to brown for 5-10 minutes, stirring. Add all other ingredients, except peas. Set pressure cooker to MEAT and give it 45 minutes. If using slow cooker transfer and set to high for 4 hours or until beef is tender.

Once this is ready, get a large bowl and strainer and separate the chunky pie filling from the liquid. Pour the liquid back into the pressure cooker and set to HIGH heat SAUTE again and let it reduce. This will become your gravy. Use a saucepan if needed, on a medium heat. Keep an eye on the gravy, stirring occasionally, to ensure it does not burn.

Once the gravy is reducing, chop the potatoes roughly and get them into a steamer. I like to leave all of the skins on my potatoes (and all other veggies where possible). Ensure you have given them a quick scrub under some water. I know this does not produce a silky mash for the topping but the skins are full of nutrients and I have come to love the chunky pieces of skin in my mash.

Stir the peas into the chunky meat that you have just strained and pop the pie filling into a casserole dish or deep pie dish then set aside. Once the potatoes are cooked, throw them into the bowl that you used to strain your filling and add a generous amount of butter. The key to good mash is butter. For this amount of potatoes, I add about 3-4 tablespoons. You could also add a little of the liquid that is reducing to make a smoother mash if you wanted less butter. Mash the potatoes until smooth and scrumptious.

The gravy may take a little while to reduce. Just keep your eye on it and once it is nice and thick pour it over the filling in your casserole dish. If you want to be fancy you can pipe the potato over the filling. If you are like me and are hungry and in a hurry then simply spread it over the filling. Pop the pie in the oven at 180°C until the potato is browned and has crispy bits on top.

Serve with greens or salad. This pie is great for leftovers and perfect for freezing.

Chapter 4

GUT GOLD

Although the gut is 'in' at the moment, it is still utterly underrated and fairly misunderstood. If we consider that there are three parts of our body that keep us alive, everyone immediately thinks of the heart and the brain, and the poor gut is forgotten. However, when conception takes place the fetus essentially starts as these three pieces of a puzzle. The rest of the body is formed from and around this, in the miraculous beginnings of a what will become a baby.

So, if evolution thinks it one of the three most important starts to life who are we to poo poo the importance of the gut. And this is exactly what has happened for the last five decades. In fact, naturopaths and herbalists have been laughed at for years for treating seemingly unrelated disorders primarily through the gut such as acne, psoriasis, thyroid disorder, infertility and so much. Now, as modern science catches up they have been shocked and impressed by how fundamental treatment of the gut can affect systemic disease states.

Our gut is not just the place where food goes. It is the control room for our immune system and contains more bugs than most people can wrap their head around. These trillions of bacteria are so different in each human that they are more unique than our fingerprints. There are at least 30% less microbes in our gut overall than we had 50 years ago. We can cure diseases by putting one person's microbes into another's, or we can make a healthy person sick with diseased microbes. The most important thing is the home that we build for these little guys to live in. If you have a leaky gut, IBS, food intolerances or allergies, skin issues, anxiety or depression, we know your gut needs some TLC. These recipes are yummy, easy to share with the kids, and will strengthen your gut blueprint.

jellies for the littles

Keep it simple- the kids will love to help make and eat these, plus they are a great daily addition to the grown ups diet thanks to all the gelatin goodness.

INGREDIENTS

- 2 tablespoons of grass fed gelatin powder
- 4 tablespoons hot water (not boiling)
- 500ml of coconut water
- Natural food dye color of your choice (optional)
- Fresh or dried fruit of your choice including berries, small bits of orange, apple, pear, apricots or sultanas
- A squeeze of lime or lemon for a zing (optional)

METHOD

Place the gelatin in a mixing bowl with a spout. Add the hot water and stir until the gelatin has dissolved. Add all of the coconut water and your food dye if you are using it and stir. Pour some of the liquid into each of your molds or into a baking paper-lined tray.

Now add whatever fruit you would like- just a few pieces in each mold or sprinkle evenly around the tray until you are satisfied. Pop them in the fridge and let them set for 4-6 hours depending on the size of your molds or thickness of gelatin in the baking tray.

This is a fun one for the kids to make themselves after you have dissolved the gelatin for them.
I have found that the berries are enough to give it vibrant color if you are unsure of using food colouring.

pineapple lollies

INGREDIENTS

- 1 cup pineapple juice
- 3 teaspoons of grass fed gelatin powder
- 1 teaspoon of honey

Optional:
- Sugar or xylitol to coat
- Powdered chili to coat (adds a punch!)

METHOD

Pop pineapple juice into a small saucepan and bring to the boil. Take off the heat and allow to slightly cool. Add honey and gelatin and whisk well until gelatin dissolves completely. Allow the mix to cool completely and pour into molds.

If you don't have molds you can cover a baking tray with plastic wrap and pour onto this. You will then need to cut into strips once it has set. Either way, pop into the fridge for a good few hours until set.

If you want to coat the lollies you can do this with plain sugar or with chili powder mixed with sugar. Pineapple and chili are best friends and the combo is worth a try. Simply roll the jollies into the sugar mix to coat them, once they have set.

frosty fruit blocks

The gelatin in these ice blocks will assist in gut healing while the pineapple is full of bromelain which is an enzyme that assists with digestion. Perfect for summer and to help the tummy after dinner. You will need ice-block molds to make these.

INGREDIENTS

- 2 tablespoons of grass fed gelatin powder
- 4 tablespoons hot water (not boiling)
- 500ml of fruit puree or juice of your choice (mango or pineapple work great, or a mix of the two!
- A squeeze of fresh lemon

METHOD

Place the gelatin in a mixing bowl with a spout. Add the hot water and stir until the gelatin has dissolved. Add the fruit juice and stir.

Pour some of the liquid into each of your molds and pop the lid on top with the sticks centered in liquid. Freeze for 4-5 hours. For some extra gut gold, add 2 tablespoons of broth to the liquid. The kids won't even know!

the perfect paddle pop

Who doesn't like a chocolate paddle pop? Gelatin assists in bringing the junctions of the gut together – like glue. While cacao is one of the highest magnesium containing foods in the world. Perfect for those with worry tummies to relax and a great replacement for after dinner sweets. You will need ice-block molds to make these.

INGREDIENTS

- 2 tablespoons of grass fed gelatin powder
- 4 tablespoons hot water (not boiling)
- 500ml of organic non-dairy milk (coconut, rice, cashew, or almond)
- 1-2 tablespoons of cacao powder, depending on how chocolatey you like it
- 1 tablespoon maple syrup or honey

METHOD

Place the gelatin in a mixing bowl with a spout. Add the hot water and stir until the gelatin has dissolved. Add the milk and stir. Add cacao and your sweetener of choice and stir together.

Pour some of the liquid into each of your molds and pop the lid on top with the sticks centered in liquid. Freeze for 4-5 hours and enjoy. For some extra gut gold, add 2 tablespoons of broth to the liquid – the kids won't even know!

homemade marshmallows

Herbalists used to make marshmallows for medicinal purposes by using the sap from the marshmallow plant. I still use marshmallow tincture in my clinic today. It is perfect for sore throats and soothing the gastrointestinal tract as it is anti-inflammatory. However, nowadays the marshmallow we buy doesn't actually contain any marshmallow itself. t is a similar situation with licorice. It is cheaper to use powdered egg, sugar, wheat and corn syrup to make these traditional treats but we lose all medicinal value. So, I wanted to show you an easy way to create healthy marshmallows at home that are good for your gut. I have left out the marshmallow itself as this is not an ingredient many people have at home but you could certainly add some if you wanted. You could also add homemade bone broth for a similar benefit. However, the gelatin will work the gut health miracle on its own.

INGREDIENTS

- 3 tablespoons of grass fed gelatin powder
- 1 cup hot water (not boiling)
- 1 cup maple syrup or honey
- ½ teaspoon salt
- 1 split vanilla bean or flavor with peppermint, lemon or orange extracts

METHOD

Use an electronic mixer for this as it needs to keep moving. In the bowl of the mixer, whisk the gelatin and half the water & set aside. In a large saucepan, place the other half of water, honey or maple syrup, and salt. Keep in mind if you choose honey your marshmallows will taste very much like honey.

This needs to get hot and have plenty of room to bubble, hence the big pot. You can use a thermometer to get it over 200°C or use the ice bowl method. Simply have a bowl of ice water next to the saucepan and when it has been boiling for 10-15 minutes start testing by putting a teaspoon of the hot liquid into the ice water and waiting until it makes a small soft ball. Do not let it go hard or your marshmallows will not be fluffy.

Remove from heat and start your mixer with the gelatin in the bowl on low, beginning to break it up. Carefully start to pour the hot syrup into the gelatin as slow as possible while the mixer is still moving on slow. Start to turn the mixer up until all the hot syrup is added and the mixer is on the highest setting.

Add your flavoring and mix for 10 minutes until it looks like the best fluffy marshmallow you have seen. Transfer the marshmallow to a lined tin. I put some pureed berries through the top of this one to give it the decoration. Set in the fridge for 6 hours or overnight and cut as desired. They will keep for a week in the fridge.

creamy custard

Who doesn't like custard? What an easy way to do some much-needed landscaping inside our digestive garden. The thing about healing the gut is that it isn't a one stop shop. In the world we live in our gut bugs are constantly under attack by our lifestyle. Stress, polluted air, poor quality food and chemical laden water all contribute to leaky gut. The mission becomes ongoing and is more about having something gut friendly each and every day, than following a strict gut healing protocol for a month. This custard can easily become a nighttime treat for the whole family and will be mowing the lawn and rebuilding the broken rock wall of your garden as you sleep.

INGREDIENTS

- 2 tablespoons of grass fed gelatin powder
- 4 tablespoons hot water (not boiling)
- 500ml of organic non-dairy milk (coconut, rice, cashew, or almond)
- 1 scraped fresh vanilla bean
- 2 tablespoons maple syrup

METHOD

Place the gelatin in a mixing bowl with a spout. Add the hot water and stir until the gelatin has dissolved. Add the remaining ingredients and combine well.

Pour some of the liquid into each of your cups. Use pretty glasses, tea cups or cute ramekins to give them a fancy vibe. Pop them in the fridge and let them set for 4-6 hours depending on the size (the larger the volume, the longer they will need).

If you want to mix things up a bit, swap the vanilla bean seeds for 2 tablespoons of cacao to make a chocolate custard or even some smashed strawberries for a strawberry custard.

drinking yoghurt

This recipe requires a good quality probiotic initially, to help begin the fermentation process. Look for one that is refrigerated and recommended by your local Naturopath if possible.

INGREDIENTS

- 1 teaspoon starter culture or food probiotics
- 2 cans full fat coconut cream
- Agar agar (optional)
- Clip lock jar with rubber seal

METHOD

Put 1 teaspoon of probiotics into a bowl and pour over 1 can of organic coconut cream. Put a tea towel over the top and leave overnight to ferment.

In the morning look and taste it. The mix should be slightly bubbled and taste sour. It may take up to 3 nights to get it to this point. Just keep checking each morning. Once it has become a sour fermented mess this will be your starter for yoghurt and anything else you want to make. Use a little in smoothies to give them an extra kick or pop some in coconut panacotta (see following page) before putting in molds.

To make yoghurt, pour a second can of coconut cream into a saucepan and heat very slowly. Bring it to a very soft simmer and take off heat straight away. Do not boil. Allow this to cool until luke warm.

Once cooled add 2 heaped tablespoons of the coconut starter. Seal this in a jar with a clip lock and rubber seal. Leave overnight in a warm dark place.

Check in the morning and taste. It may not be ready until that night or next morning depending on the weather. It should taste like Greek yoghurt. Sour and tangy with a little sweetness from the coconut.

This recipe makes a runny yoghurt which is why it is called drinking yoghurt. If you would like a thicker yoghurt you can add some agar agar but if you are happy with the drinking yoghurt just keep it simple and enjoy.

coconut panna cotta

This is a simple version to begin with. There are some really exciting and different flavor combinations out there so don't be afraid to get creative in the kitchen. Try a berry or lemon panacotta or, as I like to do, layer different things throughout the panacotta. For example, stewed apple or strawberries as a base in your mold followed by the panacotta mixture is yummy and makes a beautiful top when set and poured out. You may also like to add a little cacao powder (1-2 teaspoons) and enjoy a yummy chocolate treat.

INGREDIENTS

- 1 can full fat organic coconut milk
- 1 heaped teaspoon of gelatin
- The seeds from 1 fresh vanilla bean
- ⅓ cup maple syrup

METHOD

In a saucepan, whisk together coconut milk and gelatin. Allow to sit for 5 minutes, to bloom.

Add the vanilla, then gently heat the mixture over medium-low heat, whisking well to help the gelatin dissolve. Be careful NOT to boil this mixture.

Once the gelatin has completely dissolved, remove from the heat and stir in the maple syrup. Pour into molds or dishes, and place in the fridge to set for at least 4 hours before serving.

Chapter 5

BLEND IT

If you love smoothies than they can be an easy way to get nutrients and feed yourself on the go. They are also super easy for our gut to absorb and are almost partially digested by the blades of the blender, making them perfect for a tummy that is not working quite right as some of the work is already done.

It is a good idea to have some frozen bananas in the freezer as this gives taste, texture and a little sweetness to smoothies, as well as hides any ingredients you want to sneak in or not taste. The key to a smoothie that will sustain your energy levels is to add protein and a little fat to each one. Then you can layer in any super foods you want plus some fruit and veg.

To create a nice smooth smoothie, you need to use a liquid to bring it all together. I love using coconut water, almond milk, coconut milk from a can (adds fat) or you can always use plain old-fashioned water (filtered). Use the recipe for each smoothie as a guide for what order to add your ingredients into the blender, starting at the top and ending with your liquid.

smoothie cubes

Making smoothie cubes on a Sunday will really set you up for a successful week of eating well. Often by the end of the week we are out of fresh ingredients or they are starting to wane. So, set some time aside and gather all the ice cube trays in the house to create some smoothie cubes. You can then pop them out and store in a bowl in the freezer or in zip lock bags ready for each smoothie.

INGREDIENTS

In this photo, you can see some cubes with spinach and others with berries.

The green cubes are just whizzed up baby spinach and water but you could use kale or any other green that takes your fancy.

Optional add-ins to throw in to the smoothie in the morning: handful of nuts or seeds, a bit of bone broth, some extra spinach or fruit.

For the red cubes, I used a mix of blueberries and raspberries. I use frozen organic berries as they are just as nutritious as their fresh counterpart plus they are cheaper and go further. If you like a coconut smoothie, place half coconut milk, half berries in the cubes or freeze a tray of each. Just make sure your coconut milk is full fat, organic, in a BPA free can and has no additives or preservative (220). You can grab some from your local health food shop.

METHOD

Whiz up your chosen ingredients and pour into ice cube trays. Pop in the freezer overnight to set.

In the morning when you are ready to get your smoothie on, throw a few cubes in and top with your choice of liquid like water, dairy free milk, or coconut water, extra veggies or fruit, and a handful of nuts or seeds. Give it a good blitz and away you go.

gut gold smoothie

There are so many fancy gut healing ingredients out there now that it can be very expensive and difficult to make a simple smoothie. This one just goes to showcase the power of real food again. Using real food will deliver all the properties and medicinal benefits of the best gut healing product. This smoothie is full of anti-inflammatory foods such as ginger and turmeric to help settle a sore and bloating tummy. Omegas from chia seeds, avocado and LSA coat the mucous membranes, feeding them and giving them a chance to heal. Plus, by adding a little protein this smoothie can become the perfect breakfast or snack to keep you fueled for the day.

INGREDIENTS

- A handful each of kale, spinach and celery leaves (not stems)
- 1 tablespoon chia seeds
- 1 tablespoon LSA
- 2 tablespoons Inca Inchi protein or hemp protein
- 1 can of coconut milk
- 1 avocado
- 1 banana
- A knob of fresh ginger
- A knob of fresh turmeric

METHOD

Blend up all the ingredients and enjoy.

bug killer smoothie

This one isn't the best tasting smoothie you'll ever have but boy-oh-boy does it stop a cold in its tracks. It will also help to kill off any parasites or bugs in the gut and improve your immune fighting response. Papaya, coconut oil, lemon, Manuka and ginger are all antimicrobial, while pineapple will help to stimulate digestion and assist the gut response.

INGREDIENTS

- 1 cup papaya (pawpaw is the same thing)
- 1 cup pineapple
- 1 cup of spinach
- ½ avocado
- ½ lemon with skin on
- 1 tablespoon coconut oil
- 1-2 teaspoons Manuka honey
- Freshly grated ginger to taste
- Coconut water, enough to blend and get desired consistency

METHOD

Put fresh fruit at the bottom of the blender. Start to blend, adding other ingredients and then add in coconut water to get desired consistency. Makes enough for 2.

---

detox smoothie

One of the most common complaints I hear in clinic is bloating, and this is perfect remedy. Fennel is the ultimate digestive. It helps to stop food stagnating in the gut, which causes bloating. It also assists in weight loss by stimulating the metabolism. The rest of the greens cleanse the liver. A little ginger and lemon brings zest and zing, waking the palate and ensuring the acid in the stomach is balanced and working to break down the nutrients from our food so that they can all be absorbed.

INGREDIENTS

- 2 green apples
- 3 stalks celery, with leaves
- 2 handfuls spinach
- ½ fennel bulb, with fronds
- 1 cucumber
- 2 kale leaves, no stems
- ½ teaspoon organic ginger powder
- ½ lemon, peeled
- Water as needed

METHOD

Chop everything up so that it will fit in the blender, blend up all the ingredients, and enjoy. Serves 2.

the ultimate smoothie

This smoothie will keep you well and full. It is jammed with all the best medicinal food ingredients from brain boosting to immune bolstering, as well as being nutrient dense, blood sugar balancing, liver cleansing, alkalizing and full of antioxidants. It will replace a breakfast or lunch meal and assist with weight loss goals. You can add or take away ingredients that you do not like or have at the time and substitute for other things or just leave out. The key to an ultimate smoothie is that is has all the macronutrients: carbs, fat and protein.

INGREDIENTS

- 1 tablespoon of Raw Amazonia Protein powder
- A handful of greens (spinach, kale, rocket)
- ½ avocado
- 1 avocado seed (if your blender is strong enough)
- 2 tablespoons pepitas
- A handful of frozen berries of your choice (blueberries, strawberries, raspberries or mixed)
- 3 stalks of parsley with the full stems left on
- ¼ of a small lemon with skin on
- 3 tablespoons coconut yoghurt (or canned coconut milk)

METHOD

Add all the ingredients into your blender. Use a little extra coconut milk if you're getting it from the can, otherwise just use some water and blend it all together and enjoy.

This usually serves 1 but may be enough for 2 smoothies as a snack or if you are not a big breakfast eater.

alkalising smoothie

We all like the idea of alkalising the body as so many chronic health conditions are associated with acidity, including inflammation, but it is unclear if we can actually alkalize the body. In fact, the PH of the body is kept within a very strict range as a function of homeostasis. What we can do is provide the body with anti-inflammatory foods which will assist the liver to remove heat and reduce systemic inflammation. We know that greens are detoxifying and will therefore assist with weight loss and this smoothie is green, green, green. Enjoy anytime day or night, and with the addition of good quality protein powder this smoothie is the perfect replacement for morning or afternoon tea. If you don't have protein powder enjoy with a boiled egg or handful of nuts.

INGREDIENTS

- 1 apple or pear
- 1 handful spinach
- 1 handful kale, stem and leaves
- 1 celery stalk, with leaves
- 1 cucumber
- ½ frozen banana (take skin off before freezing)
- 1 handful of frozen berries or gojis
- 2 tablespoons of Raw Amazonian Protein Powder (optional)
- 1 or more cups of coconut water

METHOD

Chop up everything so that it will fit in the blender. No need to deseed the apple or pear. Blend cup all the ingredients and enjoy.
Serves 1.

snack smoothie

This snack smoothie can be just that, but it is also so much more. Filling and blood sugar stabilizing, it can be used as a weight loss tool to replace snacks during the day or as a replacement for dessert after dinner. It is high in protein, low in sugar and jammed with extra nutrients which will help cleanse the liver, stimulate the metabolism and fight fatigue. A little sweeter than the others, it is them perfect cure for 3:30-itis.

INGREDIENTS

- 1 cup rice or almond milk
- ½ frozen banana
- 1 teaspoon coconut oil
- 1 teaspoon chia seeds
- 1 teaspoon tahini paste
- 1 teaspoon LSA (see page 240)
- ½ cup frozen berries
- 2 kale leaves

METHOD

Blend up all the ingredients and enjoy.
Serves 2.

---

purple people eater

This smoothie is super detoxifying! Beetroot encourages our liver to clear toxins and assists with shedding excess fat, so it is great for weight loss goals. It is also full of nitric oxide (check out the glossary on page xviii for more info) so it will increase the oxygen in our blood, giving us more energy, better concentration and memory recall. This smoothie makes the perfect pre-workout an hour or so before training. And yes, purple poo is normal!

INGREDIENTS

- 2 handfuls of purple kale
- ½ apple or pear
- 2 teaspoons of food probiotics
- ¼ - ½ of 1 fresh beetroot (depending on size) cut into small cubes
- 2 cups coconut water

METHOD

Blend up all the ingredients and enjoy.

caramel smoothie

INGREDIENTS

- 2 cups almond milk
- 2 dates
- 1 banana
- 1 tablespoon cashews
- 2 scoops Amazonia Raw Salted Caramel protein
- 1 teaspoon maple syrup
- ½ cup ice

METHOD

Blend all the ingredients together and enjoy.

---

healthy snickers smoothie

INGREDIENTS

- 300 ml coconut cream or milk
- 2 dates
- 1 tablespoon extra cacao
- 1 tablespoon peanut butter
- 1 tablespoon macadamia nuts
- 2 scoops Amazonia Raw Cacao & Coconut protein powder
- 1 teaspoon each of chia seeds, hemp seeds and maca powder
- ½ cup ice

METHOD

Blend all the ingredients together and enjoy.

tumeric latte

You don't really need to blend this one but I couldn't go past a liquids sections without a healthful and fulfilling hot beverage. Turmeric is anti-inflammatory, stimulates digestion and the liver, and has been used for centuries for health benefits. It is thought to be the 'gold' that was laid at Baby Jesus' feet.

INGREDIENTS

- 2 cups of your favorite milk- almond, rice, dairy, coconut (I like Cocoquench)
- 1 vanilla bean, split and deseeded
- 1 cinnamon stick
- 1 teaspoon nutmeg
- 1 teaspoon chili flakes (optional)
- 1-2 tablespoons turmeric powder
- 1 tablespoon maple syrup

METHOD

Put all of the ingredients into a saucepan (including the vanilla bean skin) and heat over medium high heat for 15-25 minutes. Strain and enjoy straight away or pop in a stainless-steel cup to have on the go.
Serves 1.

Chapter 6

SUPER SIDES

Nothing completes a meal like an awesome side, so why not make it just as nutritious and tasty as the main part of the meal? Some of these sides can be used as meals in their own right. For example, when taking the photos Erin enjoyed the anchovy mushrooms as her lunch. They can stand alone, but will also make any meal extra special - plus add a gut healing kick! Even a simple salad can be full of flavor, well balanced and have medicinal value by assisting digestion or encouraging weight loss.

There are a few simple rules when it comes to taking a salad to the next level. Follow them to impress with your side salads:

• Always use a ridiculously huge bowl. This is not a joke. This allows room for the salad to move, mix and be coated with dressing.

• Never use tongs. They smush the ingredients and crush the life out of your greens. Use salad servers or bear claws for the best mingling effects.

• Nobody likes dry salad. There are 4 key things to good dressing. Oil, sweetness, acidity and salt. But, there also has to be enough to coat the salad and leave every piece touched by the magic.

• Add fruit and veg. By adding some apple, sultanas or orange, you raise the calibre of your salad.

• Texture is king. Fresh crisp greens, soft supple sultanas, juicy ripe tomato, crunchy cucumber, pops of nuts of seeds, velvety dressing. You get the picture.

capsicum salad

INGREDIENTS

- 5 red or yellow capsicums
- 1 bunch of fresh mint
- ½ bunch fresh parsley
- 4 tablespoons red wine vinegar
- 2 tablespoons olive oil
- ½ teaspoon of salt
- Fresh cracked pepper
- Juice of half a fresh lemon

METHOD

Blacken capsicums directly over the flame of stove or barbecue. If this does not suit you, just use a dry griddle pan or a normal frypan. Allow the skin to become black, soft and start to break away. Turn them every few minutes on each side until all skin has touched heat. Don't stress if there are patches that are missed like the tops.

Pop hot capsicums into a bowl and place a plate over the top and cover this with glad wrap. This will allow the capsicums to keep cooking and they will sweat their skin of making them easy to peel. Set them aside for 10 minutes.

Peel and scrape the majority of skin off the capsicums, leaving what doesn't budge easily and discarding the inner seeds and membranes. Tear the capsicums into fat strips and pop into a large bowl.

Shred the mint and parsley with your hands tearing into into small pieces and add it to the capsicums. Add red wine vinegar, olive oil, salt and pepper and lemon.

This salad is fantastic on its own or as a side for a main. It is especially yummy with supercharged koftas (page 209).

sweet tatie mash

Enjoy on its own, use in the bottom of a brekkie bowl with toppers like bacon & green veggies, or as an alternative to rice, pasta, or normal mash with curries & stews (like the one pot sausage & veggie stew on page 222)

INGREDIENTS

- 3 large sweet potatoes cut into chunks
- 3-4 tablespoons coconut cream, with extra to garnish
- Lots of salt & pepper to taste
- Generous pinch of cinnamon
- Generous pinch of nutmeg
- Parsley to garnish (optional)

METHOD

Steam the sweet potato chunks until soft.

Add all ingredients and mash them together until your sweet tatie is as smooth as your heart desires (I like it a little chunky). Garnish as desired.

mel's classic hummus

Plain old hummus is such an easy delicious snack for adults and kids alike. It is high in protein, good fat, fibre, iron and calcium. You can stick to the plain version or start to experiment with flavors. Hummus lends itself to an array of different flavors easily and if it is your go-to snack it's nice to spice it up sometimes.

INGREDIENTS

- 1 can of organic chickpeas, drained but save a little liquid as below
- 2 tablespoons chickpea liquid
- 1 heaped tablespoon un-hulled tahini
- Juice and zest from 1 lemon
- 1-2 cloves fresh garlic, peeled
- ¼ cup of olive oil
- ½ teaspoon sumac, and some to sprinkle on top
- Salt and pepper to taste
- 1 teaspoon sesame seeds to sprinkle on top

METHOD

Pop your chickpeas on a small oven tray and place in the oven on 180°C to warm for 5 minutes. In the meantime, blend together the tahini, lemon zest and juice, garlic, half the olive oil and sumac in your food processor.

Remove chickpeas from the oven after the 5 minutes is up and pop into a bowl to cool slightly. Add the chickpeas to the processor and whiz it all up for a minute. Add the rest of the olive oil as you blend, plus the chickpea liquid.

Taste and add salt and pepper as needed. Transfer to a warm bowl and top with extra sumac and sesame seeds. Enjoy straight away.

If you are not going to eat the hummus at the time of making, just exclude the oven components.

tumeric hummus

We all know that turmeric is the ultimate superfood spice right now. One of the key things in allowing turmeric to do all it can for our body is that it needs to be raw. Similar to garlic, once we heat it much of the medicinal properties are lost. So, this hummus allows you to get a good dose of turmeric which is still palatable. Great for the liver, anti-inflammatory and full of antioxidants.

INGREDIENTS

- 1 can of organic chickpeas, drained but save a little liquid as below
- 2 tablespoons chickpea liquid
- 1 heaped tablespoon 100% peanut butter
- Juice from 1 lemon
- 1-4 teaspoons of high grade turmeric powder
- ½ teaspoon of good quality cumin powder
- ½ teaspoon coriander powder (or 2 fresh roots – not leaves)
- Pinch of cayenne pepper (optional)
- ¼ cup and 2 tablespoons of olive oil
- Salt and pepper to taste

METHOD

Starting with 1 teaspoon of turmeric powder, place all the ingredients into a blender. Use 2 tablespoons of olive oil to start and add more as needed to help bring the ingredients together.

Blend until smooth. If it is a bit gluggy, add a little more olive oil.

Taste it right away. Check for salt, lemony-ness, turmeric flavor and texture. Add more turmeric until you're happy. Top with lots of extra olive oil and enjoy.

sun-dried tomato & mint hummus

INGREDIENTS

- 1 can organic chickpeas, drained but save ¼ cup of liquid for later
- 1-2 cloves garlic
- 1 tablespoon tahini paste
- 2 tablespoons fresh organic lemon juice
- 2-4 tablespoons olive oil
- 6-10 sun dried tomatoes
- 2 whole stalks of parsley
- a large handful of fresh mint
- 2 pinches of salt

METHOD

Add all ingredients, except extra chickpea liquid, into the food processor and blend until smooth and well combined.

Add a little chickpea juice at a time until you reach the desired consistency- you may not need it all.

Serve with some extra sun-dried tomatoes on top.

This version is also great as an olive hummus. Just swap the tomatoes for ½ cup of pitted olives.

beetroot hummus

Beetroot is a fantastic liver and kidney cleanser, and full of vitamins and minerals, especially iron. Chickpeas are high in protein so will keep you full and help maintain healthy glucose, insulin and lipid levels while warding off hunger and sweet cravings. Raw garlic is great for the cardiovascular system as well as boosting immune function.

INGREDIENTS

- 3 tablespoons black sesame seeds (or black tahini), plus seeds to sprinkle on top
- ½ large organic raw beetroot
- 1 can organic chickpeas, rinsed well and drained
- 1-2 cloves garlic
- 2 tablespoons fresh organic lemon juice
- 2-4 tablespoons olive oil
- ½ teaspoon organic cumin
- 2 pinches of salt and fresh cracked pepper

METHOD

Place black sesame seeds into the processor and blend until they become a paste. If you do not have a good processor just use tahini paste. Roughly chop the beetroot, leaving the skin on, throw into the food processor with paste and blend until fine. Add in the rest of the ingredients and blend until smooth and well combined.

No food processor? Smash up the chickpeas and grate the beetroot. Combine with remaining ingredients in a large bowl using a spatula. You may need more olive oil if doing it by hand. Enjoy!

anchovy mushrooms

Anchovies are a great source of good fats, which most of us are lacking in our diet. These oily little fish help keep us full and satiated and are great for our brain, skin, nails, hair and happiness. They also assist in keeping our cholesterol at healthy ratios and fighting heart disease and cancer by ensuring all our cells are supple and juicy. Don't be afraid of these types of wonderful fats as not having enough for the past 2 decades has had a huge impact on the rise of ill-health today. Look for anchovies in olive oil, not vegetable or soy oil. You may pay a little more but the taste is worth it.

INGREDIENTS

- 15-20 small mushrooms, sliced in half
- 1 tablespoon olive oil
- 1 clove of fresh garlic, crushed
- 1 small fresh chili, sliced
- 2 tablespoons butter
- Small handful of fresh parsley (with stems)
- Small handful of fresh chives, chopped roughly
- 5-10 anchovies (depending on how much you love them). Some whole, some halved
- Squeeze of fresh lemon to serve

METHOD

Throw the olive oil, garlic and chili in a medium hot pan and fry off for a few minutes. Bump the heat up, add the butter and the mushrooms, and cook until soft and starting to turn golden.

Throw in all your other ingredients and turn off the heat, stirring for 2 minutes or until herbs are stirred through and
anchovies are heated (they do not need to cook). I like to use anchovies which have been preserved in chili oil for this recipe but if you can't find them just add extra fresh chili at the end.

Squeeze with fresh lemon and eat right away.

quinoa tabbouleh

This fresh, crisp salad can also serve as a main as quinoa is high in protein with all the essential amino acids. It is also anti-inflamatory, packed with fibre, low carb and low GI. Combined with alkalizing parsley, this salad is made for keeping you full for longer and is perfect to assist weight loss.

INGREDIENTS

- 2 cups quinoa, cooked
- 2 bunches parsley, roughly chopped
- 250g mini roma's or cherry tomatoes, sliced in half
- 1 large cucumber, chopped into bite size pieces
- 1 cup pea shoots
- 2 lemons, juiced
- ½ cup olive oil

METHOD

Put the quinoa, parsley, tomatoes, cucumber and pea shoots into a large bowl. Add lemon juice and olive oil and toss together until well coated.

Place onto serving platter piled up high.

roast beet & quinoa salad

This colourful salad will have your dinner guests impressed. With deep purple wedges and pops of bright pink pomegranate this simple but delicious salad will become a favourite for family events.

INGREDIENTS

- 4 beetroots
- 6 tablespoons olive oil
- 2 cups quinoa, cooked
- 1 bunch of mint, chopped roughly
- The leaves of the beetroot, washed well and chopped roughly
- Juice of 1 lemon
- 1 pomegranate

METHOD

Chop the beetroots into quarters and place on an oven tray. Drizzle over half the olive oil and toss the beetroots so they are coated. Place in the oven on 180°C for 45 minutes or until a fork goes in easily. Once cooked set them aside to cool.

Place quinoa, beetroot leaves, mint and lemon juice into a bowl and toss together. Add cooled beetroot and transfer the salad to a serving platter before adding pomegranate. Slice pomegranate in half and use a wooden spoon to bash the seeds out directly onto the salad, including any juice that comes out. I like to squeeze the skin as much as possible to release any leftover juice after bashing the seeds out as well.

Drizzle with the rest of the olive oil. Serve with more freshly sliced lemons.

healthy coleslaw with pomegranate dressing

Once you have had homemade coleslaw dressing you will never buy it from the shop again. Not only is it very easy but it is so much more enjoyable to the taste buds. This way you also get all the benefits of raw egg plus you can choose the oil you use, keep it preservative free and add pops of color and flavor like pomegranate. I have super charged a simple cabbage slaw into a nutrient dense vitamin and mineral storage house with loads of fresh additions and seeds. Seeds are packed with micronutrients including loads of calcium for our bones.

INGREDIENTS

- ½ green cabbage, shredded
- ½ purple cabbage, shredded
- 1 bunch kale, shredded
- 2 carrots, grated
- 4 tablespoons sesame seeds
- 4 tablespoons hemp seeds
- 4 tablespoons pepita (pumpkin) seeds

For the dressing:
- 1 pomegranate
- 1 cup homemade mayo (page 246)
- ½ teaspoon Dijon mustard
- ½ teaspoon salt
- fresh cracked pepper

METHOD

You need a really big bowl for this one so that all the cabbage can be coated in dressing. Remember cabbage triples in size once cut. Add all ingredients for the salad into the big bowl and toss it together.

Slice the pomegranate and set one half aside for decorating the top of the salad. Use a wooden spoon to bash the seeds from the other half into the mayo including any juice that you can get out of it. Add the extra mustard, salt and pepper to the mayo and stir. Pour into the coleslaw and toss to dress well. Transfer to serving platter and using the wooden spoon again, bash the leftover pomegranate seeds onto the salad.

Serve with fresh lemon wedges.

lemon & fennel salad

The perfect side to a heavy dish as it is light, fresh and a pure digestive. Fennel is used medicinally to calm and relax the tummy, while helping food to digest and breakdown. With the addition of lemon this salad will brighten your palate and change the way your tummy sees food. Traditionally fennel was used to treat colic in babies and I still use it in the clinic for bloating and IBS. Enjoy this one knowing it is food serving as medicine.

INGREDIENTS

- 1 fennel bulb
- 1 lemon
- A handful of fresh herbs- mint or parsley work well (or try both)
- A nice big slosh of olive oil to coat
- 1 tablespoon red wine vinegar
- Salt and pepper to taste

METHOD

You will need a food processor to get the right consistency for this salad. Cut the fronds (hairy ends) off the bulb of fennel and set aside. Clean off the end and any outer leaves as needed. Put through the food processor, slicing with a fine blade on and set aside in a large salad bowl. Next slice the lemon in half and put it through the food processor as well, skin on.

Add the sliced lemon to the bowl with the fennel and coat with olive oil, red wine vinegar and a generous amount of salt and pepper. Break apart some of the fennel fronds and add to the bowl as well. Roughly chop herbs and add. Toss it all together and place on a serving platter.

Decorate with extra fronds and black pepper and serve immediately.

cashew cheese

This is so simple and super tasty, plus you can really make it whatever you want by changing a few simple things. Make chunky cashew cheese topper or dip, or blend it a bit longer to get a smooth cheese like Philly.

INGREDIENTS

- 2 cups of raw cashews
- 2 tablespoons nutritional yeast
- ¼ cup filtered water
- Juice of 1 lemon
- A good pinch of salt

METHOD

Blend all ingredients together until desired consistency.

This will keep in the fridge for up to a week.

Try different flavor combinations such as adding a mixture of herbs for herbed cashew cheese, chili for a spicy cheese or spices such as turmeric for a change.

---

cashew cream

As with cashew cheese, this is so simple and super tasty. Again, you can change the end product each time by simply adding a different fruit. From vanilla and pear, to apple and cinnamon, the opportunities for a yummy and wholesome dessert are endless.

INGREDIENTS

- 1 cup raw cashews (or try a different nut or seed such as almonds or sunflower seeds)
- ½ cup canned apricots or stewed apples or pears
- The seeds of 1 fresh vanilla pod

METHOD

Blend all ingredients until super smooth.

You can add a little extra fruit juice if the mix is dry.

This mix will keep in the fridge for 1 week (if you're lucky and the kids don't find it) and can be used as an accompaniment to any dessert or just on its own.

paleo snack mix

This will usually last about a week (depending on how much you eat.)

INGREDIENTS

- 1 cup organic raw almonds
- 1 cup organic raw cashews
- 1 cup organic raw walnuts
- ½ cup organic raw brazil nuts
- ½ cup raw pepitas
- ½ cup organic raw sunflower seeds
- ½ cup organic naturally sweetened dried cranberries
- 1 cup organic dried goji berries
- 1 cup organic coconut flakes
- 2 pinches of Himalayan crystal salt

METHOD

Combine all the ingredients and you're good to go.

scrummy snack muffins

INGREDIENTS

- 6 eggs
- 1 ½ cup LSA
- 1 cup coconut milk
- 1 teaspoon cumin
- 1 teaspoon paprika
- A handful of diced bacon
- A handful of diced capsicum
- A handful of fresh parsley

METHOD

Preheat the oven to 180° and grease a muffin tin with coconut oil.

Whisk the eggs in a bowl with the LSA, milk, spices, bacon, capsicum, and parsley.

Pour batter into the muffin tins and bake for 35-40 minutes, depending on the size of your muffin trays. Keep an eye on them. They are ready when browned on top and are no longer runny or wet.

seed balls

INGREDIENTS

- 1 cup pepitas
- 1 cup sunflower seeds
- ¼ cup sesame seeds
- 4-10 medjool dates (depending on sweet tooth) or none at all
- 1 ½ cups coconut oil, maybe more
- ½ cup ghee (optional)
- ½ cup chia seeds
- 1 teaspoon vanilla bean paste
- 1 tablespoon organic powdered cinnamon
- ½ cup cacao powder
- ½ cup goji berries
- Generous pinch of pink salt
- Optional: dash of honey or maple syrup to help convince the kids to eat them

METHOD

Pulse the pepitas, sunflower seeds, sesame seeds, and dates in a food processor until powdery but still lumpy. Place aside in a large bowl. Start to melt the coconut oil and ghee in a small sauce pan over very low heat. Turn off when half melted and leave the rest to melt away from heat. Stir periodically.

Place all other ingredients into the bowl with the seed & date mix. Start to add the coconut oil and ghee with one hand, mixing it through with the other hand. You want to add enough liquid so that you can start to squeeze the mix together and it keeps its shape. Coconut oil will go hard once in the fridge and set the balls, but you need to be able to roll them. Too wet will smush them, too dry and they'll fall apart.

I personally hate rolling balls so I love pressing the mix into a tray and just cutting it like a slice once it has set.

lemon & double maca balls

INGREDIENTS

- 1 cup cashews
- 1 cup macadamias
- 2 TB maca powder
- 3 medjool dates (pitted)
- 1 good pinch salt
- 1 lemon, zest and juice
- ½ cup shredded coconut
- 1 tablespoon maple syrup or honey

METHOD

Whiz all ingredients up in a food processor until it comes together.

If you prefer you can skip the rolling and just press the mixture into a lined baking tin. Pop your balls or pressed slice into the fridge to set. They will last for 1 week refrigerated.

BETTER BREADS

There's no better side than fresh made bread. We just need to raise the quality of the bread we are eating and lessen the quantity. Remember, there are no 'good' nor 'bad' foods. Foods are just foods and they only become harmful when we do not eat them in moderation, or they are far removed from what they used to be.

This is the case with the luscious, soft white bread that lasts for weeks without developing any mold. This type of bread is extremely high in refined sugars (which is why it doesn't rot) and the wheat used has not undergone any fermentation making it quite harsh on the digestive system and contributing to allergies and intolerance.

Try these homemade breads instead and feel the difference inside your tummy and out.

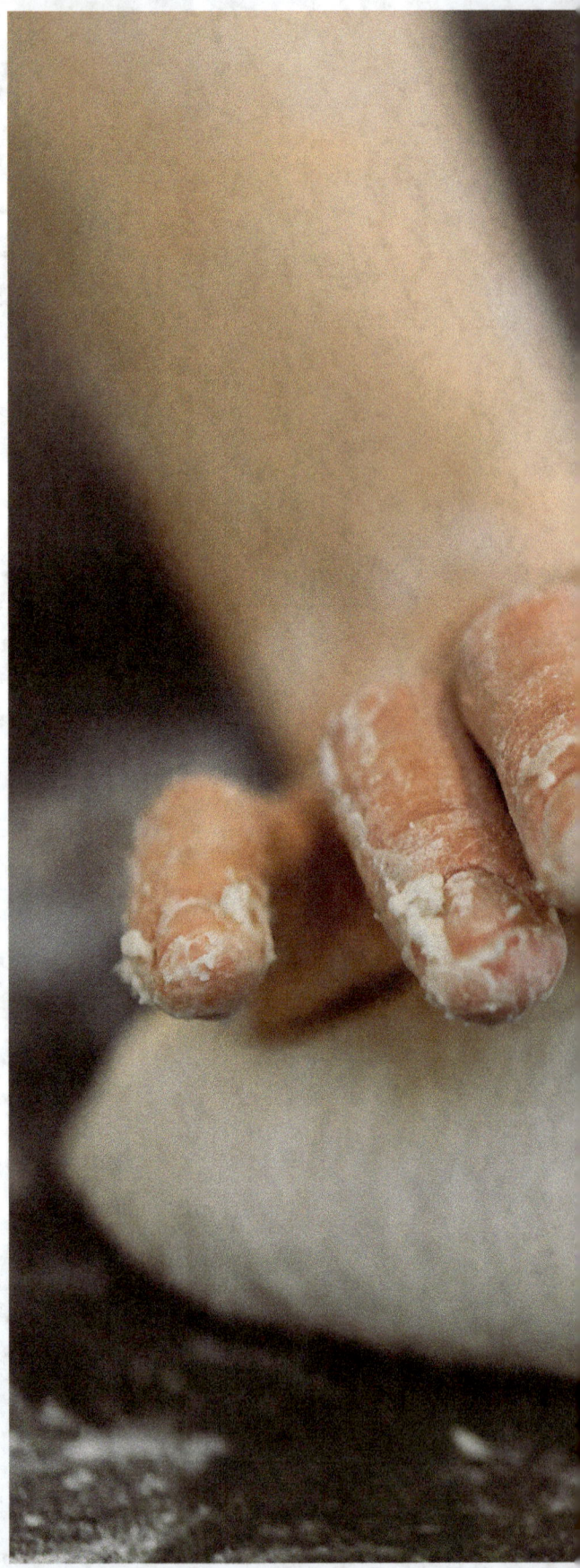

nutty seedy life changing bread

LSA is a blend of ground linseeds (flax seeds), sunflower seeds, and almonds. This mix is an amazing source of dietary fiber, protein, omega fatty acids, minerals, and vitamins. You can purchase pre-mixed LSA at health food stores, or make it yourself (see the LSA recipe on page 240). This bread is a no-fail recipe. I often change the ingredients adding different nuts and seeds and it always works well. You can even make it sweet by using hazelnuts instead of almonds and adding a banana.

INGREDIENTS

- 3 tablespoons sunflower or hemp seeds
- 3 tablespoons pumpkin seeds
- 1 tablespoon chia seeds
- 1 tablespoon quinoa seeds
- 3 tablespoons almonds, whole
- 2 tablespoons cashews
- 1 cup almond meal
- 1 cup LSA
- 1 teaspoon bicarbonate of soda
- 2 tablespoons coconut flour
- 6 eggs
- 1 tablespoon raw apple cider vinegar
- 4 tablespoons coconut oil, melted
- 1 teaspoon Himalayan crystal salt

METHOD

Preheat the oven to 160°C. Grease a loaf tin with some coconut oil.

Roughly chop and mix all the seeds with the nuts, almond meal, LSA, bicarb, and coconut flour. Add the eggs, vinegar, coconut oil, and salt, and mix well to combine. Pour the batter into the loaf tin and sprinkle some extra seeds on top if you wish.

Bake for 45-50 minutes, or until golden and a knife comes out clean. Allow time to cool in the tin before turning out.

sourdough starter

To make sourdough you need to first make a leaven or starter culture and this takes a week or so at first, but you need never do it again if you look after it. The older the leaven, the stronger the strains of bacteria, and the yummier the bread (in my opinion). The reason sourdough bread has all those holes throughout it is because of the leaven. As the bread rises, the gases from the fermentation create the pockets of air. Different bacteria and yeasts give different flavor, but the most common thing you will taste from true sourdough is the sourness.

So, what is leaven? Simply water and flour. The bacteria we are talking about is found on the surface of the grains such as wheat, rye, spelt and rice. We can also cheat a little to ease the progression of fermentation with things like dried fruit, yoghurt and food probiotics. This gives the bacteria and yeast more food (sugar) and extra bugs to colonize creating a stronger ferment.

INGREDIENTS

- Gluten free flour
- Room temperature water
- Organic sultanas (optional)
- Clip lock jar

METHOD

Before making bread, we must make the starter. This will take 6 days initially.

Begin your sourdough starter in a medium clicklock jar with a rubber seal. You can use wheat flour here if you prefer but I have given you a gluten free loaf recipe. Ensure you get a mix of gluten free flours to achieve a successful loaf of bread. I just buy this pre-made but you can mix your own if you wish. It is difficult to get the right consistency with gluten free flours so getting it pre-made takes out the issue of the bread not forming. As long as it is organic with no additives it will work perfectly.

Combine ½ cup flour and ½ cup of water. Whisk it up and pop the lid on loosely. I like to throw in a few organic sultanas just to help the ferment.

For the next 6 days, add ½ cup more flour and ½ cup of water each morning. Mix it up and reseal. Repeat and keep an eye on your starter. You may notice some liquid form at the top- this is fine and normal. Just mix it in when you are re-feeding each day. If you do not see any bubbles after 2 days then add a few more sultanas. From day 6 onwards, you will be ready to make bread or sourdough pancakes.

Each time you take some of the starter out for creating goodies, you need to replace an equivalent amount of flour and water. This will save you having to start again and will keep your starter alive. For example, if you take out 1 cup of starter, add ½ cup flour and ½ cup of water back in.

FOR KEEPING:

if you use it every few days, the starter can live on the bench. Remember that each time you re-feed you need to give the starter 2 days before using again. This is known as keeping the starter active.

If you would like to store the leaven, are not using it for a few days, or are going away, pop it in the fridge. The starter will separate, but don't be concerned as this is normal. To revive the starter after refrigeration, drain the liquid from the top and use the bottom half of the starter. Add to this 1 cup of flour and 1 cup of water. Leave for 24 hours and repeat, leaving for another 24 hours. Your mix should be bubbling and alive again by now. If not, you may need to begin again.

rustic sourdough bread

Sourdough is the ultimate of breads. There are many who believe that we should not be eating wheat at all unless it has been fermented to remove the 'anti-nutrients' which are present. Unfermented wheat is blamed for the common issue of wheat and gluten intolerance and sensitivity. Traditionally, wheat was always fermented as this was the only way to create bread. All bread was a sourdough of sorts. Now we have bagged bread being made and sold within hours of that wheat being harvested.

INGREDIENTS

- 3 ½ cups gluten free flour
- ¼ cup flaxseed meal
- 1 tablespoon salt
- A pinch of sugar
- ⅓ cup soft butter
- 1 chia egg (see page 240) or 2 tablespoons xanthan gum
- 4 eggs
- 2 cups of your homemade starter
- ⅔ cup water

METHOD

Mix all dry ingredients in the bowl of a mix master or if doing by hand in a large bowl. Add the water and start on a low speed as you slowly add all the other wet ingredients, one at a time.

Turn the mixer up to medium and allow all ingredients to combine, stopping and scraping down sides as needed. Do not over blend. As soon as the mix has come together take it out of the mixer and place into a clean bowl with a sprinkle more flour to stop it sticking. You do not need to knead this dough. Set aside with a tea towel on top overnight and allow the dough to ferment and rise.

When ready to bake, preheat oven to 200°C. Carefully pour sourdough out of bowl onto a flat tray, lined with paper to stop it sticking. Place into the hot oven and allow to cook for 30-40 minutes. You will know it is cooked through when you can tap it and it sounds hollow, or just by looking at the golden crispy crust that has developed.

Let your bread cool before slicing. I know it's hard, but it's worth the wait. Slather in butter, enjoy and try to share.

Part 2
Every Day Family Meals

Chapter 7
RISE & SHINE

green omelette

INGREDIENTS

- 4 eggs
- ¼ cup almond milk
- A knob of butter
- Handful of spinach, chopped roughly
- ½ apple, sliced thinly
- Salt and pepper
- Parsley to garnish

METHOD

Crack eggs into a bowl and whisk them together along with milk. Throw the butter into a small frypan over medium heat and pour in egg mixture. Give it 2-3 minutes before sprinkling spinach over the top and then placing avocado and apple alternately around as pictured.

Allow the egg to cook through and try to get out and onto a plate in one piece.
op with fresh parsley, salt and cracked pepper to serve. Serves 2.

tomato & mushroom foldover

INGREDIENTS

- 4 eggs
- ¼ cup almond milk
- A knob of butter
- 4 mushrooms, sliced thinly
- 6 cherry or baby roma tomatoes, chopped into halves

METHOD

Crack eggs into a bowl and whisk them together with along milk. Throw the butter into a small frypan over medium heat and pour in egg mixture. Spread mushrooms and tomatoes over the egg mix and allow to cook for 2-3 minutes before folding the omelette in half. Allow to cook through for another few minutes and enjoy.

leftover hash

When I was little my Nan always used to make Bubble & Squeak. She would not let any food waste and we would eat these types of hash until all the food was used up. Leftover hash is all about what you have left over from the night before. Sometimes we have a few meals worth of leftovers which is always exciting as I can put loads of different things in. They key is to have some kind of mash to keep it all together. Here is a recipe to get you started but please do stray and include what you have at the time.

INGREDIENTS

- 1 zucchini (this one was sliced thickly and fried from the night before)
- 1 cup of pulled meat (leftover beef short ribs - page 50 - are pictured)
- 2 cups of sweet potato mash
- Salt and pepper to taste

METHOD

Warm the meat and zucchini through in a frypan before adding mash.
Push the mash into the frypan and allow it to form a crust on the bottom as it heats.

chia pudding

INGREDIENTS

- 1 cup of your choice of liquid (water, dairy/ non-dairy milks, etc.)
- 4 tablespoons chia seeds

METHOD

Mix your choice of liquid with the chia seeds and pop in the fridge overnight to set.

FLAVOUR OPTIONS

Here are some suggested add-ins, but feel free to switch it up and have a little fun with it.

ChocChoc:
2 tablespoons cacao powder and 1 tablespoon maple syrup

Banarama:
½ banana, smashed seeds of 1 vanilla pod and 1 teaspoon honey

Vanilla Coconut:
Use coconut cream as your liquid, add the seeds of 1 vanilla pod and sweeten to your taste.

Fresh Fruit:
Dice up some fresh fruit of your choice and add to the mix.

Tropical Pudding:
Add in mango, fresh coconut flesh, and passionfruit seeds for a tropical twist.

crunchy nutty no grain-ola

Want a nut-free granola? Swap out the mixed nuts for equal amounts pepitas, sunflower seeds, sesame seeds, flaxseeds, or a mix of them all. The chia seeds and sesame seeds in this will give you a solid boost of calcium.

INGREDIENTS

- 3 tablespoons coconut oil, butter, or ghee
- 2 cups coconut flakes
- 2 cups unsalted nuts and/or seeds (mix it up with macadamias, walnuts or cashews. I like to do 1 cup cashews and 1 cup of mixed pepitas and sunflower seeds)
- 2 tablespoons chia seeds
- 1 teaspoon sesame seeds
- 1 teaspoon ground cinnamon (optional)
- ¼ cup honey
- ½ cup full-fat natural yoghurt or coconut yoghurt (to serve)

METHOD

Combine all the ingredients, except serving yoghurt, in a large bowl. Mix well to coat with honey. Transfer to the baking tray and spread evenly. Bake for about 20-25 minutes until golden, turning halfway through the cooking time. The darker it is, the crunchier it will be.

Remove from the oven and allow to cool. Store it in an airtight container in the pantry for cup to 2 weeks, or in the freezer for even longer.

chocolate granola

Cacao is full of magnesium making this granola a great way to feed your nervous system whilst feeding your soul. Such a nice alternative to sugar laden breakfast cereals for the kids as well.

INGREDIENTS

- 3 tablespoons coconut oil, butter, or ghee
- 2 cups coconut flakes
- 1 cup hazelnuts
- 1 cup mixed seeds (pepitas, sunflower)
- 2 tablespoons chia seeds
- 1 teaspoon sesame seeds
- 3 tablespoons of raw cacao powder
- ¼ cup honey
- ½ cup full-fat natural yoghurt or coconut yoghurt and fresh fruit (to serve)

METHOD

Preheat oven to 120°C and line a baking tray with baking paper. Combine all the ingredients, except yoghurt and fruit in a large bowl. Spread the mixture out evenly on the tray.

Bake for about 20-25 minutes until golden, turning halfway through the cooking time. The darker it is, the crunchier it will be. Remove from the oven and allow to cool.

Store it in an airtight container in the pantry for cup to 2 weeks, or in the freezer for even longer.

glamping eggs

Don't be scared off by the idea of camping! These eggs are so easy they can be cooked while camping or are perfect for a morning brekkie before work as well. They are easy but super tasty and will keep you going all day. By adding rosemary and coriander, you increase the body's ability to detox while stimulating the metabolism. You are also feeding yourself a high protein breakfast to start the day which will stabilize blood sugar levels and keep you full for longer, curbing any morning tea cake cravings.

INGREDIENTS

- 3 tablespoons olive oil
- 1 medium tub of mixed small tomatoes
- 3 fresh sprigs of rosemary
- 4 eggs
- 4 tablespoons fresh yoghurt
- Handful fresh coriander

METHOD

Drizzle the olive oil into a medium sized fry pan and throw the tomatoes in whole. Crank the heat up and as the tomatoes start to get hot, poke them with a knife a few times so they burst open a little.

Add rosemary and cook until soft and still juicy. Make space for eggs and crack them into the pan. Let them cook to your desired amount (I like mine runny) and serve in the pan topped with yoghurt and fresh coriander.

Season with a little salt and fresh cracked pepper just before you are about to dig in.

break-fast muffins

Have these little babies ready to grab and run. Mix it up and swap the mushrooms for your favorite vegetable, or try some cooked pumpkin or sweet potato.

INGREDIENTS

- 6 eggs
- ¾ cup LSA (see pg. 276 for recipe)
- 1 cup almond milk
- ½ cup mushrooms
- 1 handful of spinach
- 1-2 cooked chicken thighs, chopped roughly
- Herbs to flavor such as fresh basil, parsley or thyme, or dried cumin or paprika
- ½ cup full fat feta cheese, broken up (optional)

METHOD

Preheat oven to 180°C. Grease a muffin baking tray or pop in some muffin liners.

Whisk the eggs in a large bowl, and add in the rest of the ingredients. Mix well. If your mixture is too wet, add a little more LSA. Divide the mixture between the muffin tray, leaving a little room at the top for them to rise.

Bake in the oven for 35 minutes, or until a butter knife comes out clean. Store in the fridge or freezer in zip lock bags, ready to grab and go.

coconut pancakes

A healthy and easy breakfast option for the kids. Change it up – minus the spices and add some lemon or lime zest to the mix for a different spin. Or, try savory pancakes by taking away the spices and adding a handful of corn kernels, teaspoon of cumin and paprika, and topping with cottage cheese and fresh coriander.

INGREDIENTS

- 5 eggs
- ¾ cup coconut flour
- ½-1 cup coconut cream, cashew milk, or almond milk (enough to get a smooth pancake batter)
- 2 teaspoons cinnamon
- 2 teaspoons nutmeg
- 1 teaspoon ground ginger
- 1-2 teaspoons maple syrup to taste (or your favorite liquid sweetener)
- Coconut oil, ghee, or butter to fry in
- Fresh fruit, coconut yoghurt, and extra maple syrup to serve

METHOD

Add the eggs and the coconut flour to a bowl and whisk together until smooth. Add coconut cream by the tablespoon to form a thick batter. You may not need the entire cup of liquid depending on the size of your eggs. Add the spices.

Heat a frying pan with coconut oil over medium-high heat. Pour in batter to make pancakes in batches without over-crowding the pan. Small pancakes as pictured work best. Add more oil as needed.

Once finished, drizzle over some maple syrup, add a dollop of coconut yoghurt, and garnish with some fresh fruit of your choice.

Chapter 8
LUNCH BREAK

detox soup

Green means good. Good for the heart, the liver, skin and high in iron. This soup is also full of calcium, vitamin K, folic acid, beta carotene, antioxidants and will help fight cancer and reduce risk of heart disease. By stimulating the phase 2 path in the liver, this soup will allow the body to take toxins out from the body and assist with maintain a healthy weight range.

INGREDIENTS

- 2 white onions, chopped roughly
- 6 cloves of garlic, peeled and smashed
- 3 tablespoons olive oil
- 1 zucchini, chopped roughly
- 2 carrots, chopped roughly
- 1 bunch of parsley, including stalks, chopped in half
- 1 broccoli, head and stalk, chopped roughly
- 1 cauliflower, head and stalk, chopped roughly
- 5 cups of broth or enough to cover vegetables
- Loads of salt and pepper
- Hazelnut oil, ½ lemon and a handful of chopped hazelnuts to serve

METHOD

Place the onion and garlic into a very large heavy based broth pot or saucepan with olive oil. Cook off for 5 minutes until translucent. Add all other vegetables and broth. Ensure the vegetables are all covered with liquid.

Add plenty of salt and pepper to taste and bring to the boil. Reduce to a simmer and cover. Cook for 1 hour, stirring occasionally, until a knife goes though the harder veggies (broccoli stalk) easily.

Once cooled slightly, use a hand blender to make a smooth puree. Add more stock to get desired texture.

To serve, heat soup through then top with garnishes. Drizzle hazelnut oil over the top and squeeze fresh lemon, sprinkle chopped hazelnuts to add crunch and enjoy.

Serves 4—plus lunches.

buddha bowl

Buddha bowls are an easy and nourishing way to start your day or to prep as lunch. They are similar to traditional Chinese and Japanese dishes and the principles of a macro bowl. The well-loved Korean Bibimbap is a popular way to use up leftovers and provide an easy, healthy meal and literally means mixed rice. The idea is that you take a bowl, start with a grain, top with meat and add a mixture of cooked and raw veg. Add an egg and spicy sauce or hummus and you have the perfect feast all rolled into one. The thing to remember when following a recipe for a Buddha bowl is that there is no recipe. It is all about what you have at home and I love the idea of reducing our food waste by throwing it all in together for the next meal. This is my modern take on my Nanna's bubble and squeak. Even though you don't need any instructions here are some ideas to get you started and my favorite inclusions.

INGREDIENTS

- 1 cup of quinoa, cooked
- ½ cup chopped capsicum, raw
- ½ cup grated carrot
- 6 broccoli florets with stems, lightly blanched or fried
- ½ avocado, sliced
- ½ cup raw zucchini, cut into sticks or peeled into ribbons
- A few tablespoons of chunky cashew cheese to top
- ½ fresh lemon, sliced to squeeze on before eating
- Optional- top with a boiled egg, smoked salmon or a few good quality sardines

METHOD

Prep all ingredients and half into 2 serving bowls or re-usable containers for lunch prep.

Enjoy for breakfast, lunch or dinner.

Some other ingredients you could try in a buddah bowl include homemade hummus or spicy homemade Kim Chi. You can use any veg that takes your fancy and you may like to cook some and leave others fresh for different textures. I have used quinoa as a base but you could use mashed sweet tatie, brown rice, lentils or a mix.

weed salad with citrus segments

INGREDIENTS

- 2 large handfuls of fresh weeds – this can include local rocket, dandelion leaves, chickweed, onion flowers or whatever you can source locally. Pictured are Italian dandelion, rocket, mixed lettuce, pea shoots, nasturtium leaves and flowers an array of micro herbs and edible flowers.

- 1 ruby grapefruit, plus juices
- 2 oranges, plus juices
- 2 tablespoons olive oil

METHOD

Wash and dry the weeds and place in a large bowl. Keep any flowers aside for garnish.

Segment the grapefruit and oranges so that all the bitterness is removed. To do this, first cut the bottom and top off so you have a flat base to work on, then peel them whole. Set the peels aside to squeeze over the salad after its put together. Remove any remaining white pith. Now simply cut between the membranes to bring out each segment individually. Throw the segments into the salad and scrape juice form the board as you go.

Squeeze the peels over the top of the salad and drizzle with olive oil.
Decorate with flowers and enjoy immediately.

potato salad with olives & miso dressing

INGREDIENTS

- 1kg small white or mixed potatoes
- 1 bunch parsley, roughly chopped
- 200g mixed olives, pitted
- 250g cherry tomatoes, halved
- 1 red onion, sliced thinly
- 1 fresh red capsicum, chopped roughly
- ¼ cup red wine vinegar
- 2 tablespoons of miso paste
- 2-3 teaspoons maple syrup
- ¼ cup olive oil
- Fresh cracked pepper

METHOD

If potatoes are a bite size then cook whole. If they are larger than cut into even chunks. Steam for 10 minutes or until a knife goes through easily. Be sure not to over-cook so that the potatoes break when you touch them.

While the potatoes are cooking, start chopping the other ingredients. Into a very big bowl mix together parsley, olives, tomatoes, onion and capsicum. Once potatoes are cooked through, run cold water over them and set them aside to cool. Once they are room temperature you can add them to the rest of the ingredients in the bowl. Do not add before they are cooled or they will wilt your fresh ingredients.

To make the dressing simply place the vinegar, miso, maple syrup, olive oil, and pepper into a small glass jar and shake well. Taste to see if it needs more salt (keep in mind miso is quite salty). Dress the salad just before serving.

You can cook the potatoes and prep the fresh ingredients the day before and put together when serving.

kale, quinoa & roast veg salad

This makes a large salad as pictured & will keep for 3 days in the fridge.

INGREDIENTS

- 4 potatoes
- 1 medium sweet potato
- ½ small pumpkin
- 1 bunch of Dutch carrots
- 1 bunch of kale
- 4 tablespoons olive oil
- 2 tablespoons apple cider vinegar
- 1 bunch of fresh parsley
- 1 bunch of fresh mint
- 1 pomegranate
- 1 cup quinoa, cooked
- 2 lemons

METHOD

Wash, cut, and roast the potatoes, pumpkin, and carrots in bite-sized pieces and pop aside to cool. This can be done ahead of time and the veg stored in the fridge for up to 3 days prior to making the salad. Chop the kale roughly and rinse, then put it into a large salad bowl. Add the olive oil, apple cider vinegar and some salt and pepper. Get your hands into the kale and massage it until it is soft and bright green.

Roughly chop up the fresh herbs (including the stems) and add to the kale. Cut the pomegranate in half and bash it on the backside over the kale to propel the seeds and juice into the salad. Add in the cooled roast veggies plus the quinoa. Mix well to combine.

Garnish and serve with fresh lemon wedges.

chicken nuggets

These are great for school lunches, or as an extra protein topper on a salad.

INGREDIENTS

- Chicken thighs, cut into bite sized pieces as picture
- Tapioca flour
- Herbs
- Spices (try cumin & paprika)
- Chia seeds and/or sesame seeds (for crunch)
- Enough coconut oil or ghee to fry

METHOD

Coat the chicken thighs in a blend of tapioca flour, herbs & spices, chia seeds and/or sesame seeds. Fry them up in coconut oil or ghee.

Enjoy on their own, or throw atop a salad for a quick yet filling meal.

mel's chicken & avo salad with homemade ranch dressing

INGREDIENTS

Ingredients for Salad:
- 2 organic chicken breasts, poached or fried in oil
- 2-3 large handfuls of mixed greens
- 1 bunch of asparagus, lightly blanched or flash fried in oil
- 1 bunch of broccolini, lightly blanched or flash fried in oil
- 1 large handful of snow peas, topped and tailed
- 2 tablespoons wakame flakes
- 2-4 tablespoons raw organic pepitas
- 1 handful raw organic cashews

Ingredients for Dressing:
- 1 avocado, mashed
- 2 tablespoons oil
- 2 tablespoons coconut cream
- 1 tablespoon Bragg's apple cider vinegar
- 1 tablespoon parsley
- 1 teaspoon Dijon mustard

METHOD

To make the ranch dressing, mix together the avocado, coconut oil, coconut cream, vinegar, parsley, Dijon, and a pinch of salt and pepper to taste.

Add all of the salad ingredients together in a large bowl. Drizzle over the ranch dressing and enjoy.

pumpkin & spinach frittata

Being a colorful veg, pumpkin is packed with antioxidants such as Vitamin C and E, as well as B vitamins, iron and magnesium. Plus, the addition of baby spinach makes this dish a great detoxifier. Full of protein, these frittata's will keep you full and assist with weight loss goals when enjoyed for lunch or an afternoon snack.

INGREDIENTS

- 6 eggs
- A splash of milk (dairy, almond or cashew work well)
- 1 cup of baby spinach, roughly chopped
- ½ teaspoon cumin power
- ½ teaspoon salt
- Fresh cracked pepper
- 2 cups pumpkin, cubed and roasted

METHOD

Preheat oven to 170°C. Grease or line 6 small muffin or cupcake tray holes. In a large bowl, crack all the eggs and add the milk, spinach, cumin, salt and pepper. Whisk well to combine.

Divide the mix into the tray filling only ⅔ of the way up. Add 5-6 cubes of pumpkin to each of the mixes. Place into the oven for around 25 minutes or until the egg feels firm when quickly pressed (don't burn your fingers.).

Enjoy as a super easy, nutritious and tasty lunch with salad or veg, hot or cold.

pumpkin soup

Pumpkin soup is nutritious, delicious and super easy. There is no need to laden it with cream for flavor if you treat the pumpkin right from the start. The pumpkin is packed with the nutrients described in the frittata plus you have the opportunity to use some of the beautiful bone broth. Start by using a whole pumpkin. It is much more economical, tastes better fresh, plus you can do so much with it. Scoop the seeds out and roast them separately with a little salt for a crunchy snack later.

INGREDIENTS

- ½ a pumpkin of your choice—kent or butternut are my fav's
- 6 tablespoons of olive oil
- 2 teaspoons of cinnamon
- 2-3 cups bone broth or you can use the Asian poached chicken liquid, giving your soup a spicy twist
- 1 bulb of garlic, whole
- 1 handful or coriander, chopped roughly
- 1 handful of cashews, chopped roughly (or you can use cashew cheese or cream if you have some made up)
- Salt and pepper to taste

METHOD

Get a large oven tray ready and preheat the oven to 170°C.

Chop the pumpkin into large pieces, leaving the skin on. Place it in a large bowl and toss in olive oil and cinnamon. Ensure you coat every piece evenly. This is a job that only your hands can do well. Arrange the pumpkin on the oven tray with room for it to move. Use a second tray if needed.

Chop the pinnacle top off the garlic, just slicing through the top of some of the cloves and place on the oven tray as well. Bake in the oven for at least an hour or until pumpkin has a little color and is super soft and tender.

Remove and allow pumpkin to cool slightly before transferring to a food processor or back to a large bowl if using a hand blender. Squeeze the soft garlic from the bulb of cloves into the pumpkin mix. Lick your fingers.

Add ½ the stock and start to bring together. Add more stock until it reaches your desired consistency. Serve hot topped with fresh coriander and cashews on top. Add salt and pepper to taste.

Chapter 9
THE MAIN EVENT

sammy's biksemad

This Danish hash came into my life through a heart-breaking loss for my husband. Sadly, I did not get to meet its cook but each time Sam recreates it, I feel a little of his spirit in this special dish. It allows us to be grateful for what we have and to fondly reflect. Biksemad means 'food that has been mixed together' and many cultures do this with leftovers. I would extend this meaning to 'food that mixes people together' as these traditional dishes are often family staples and favorites laced with sentimentality. I have added my own twist by using pork neck in this recipe. A seldom used cut of pork which holds so much flavor and untapped talent. However, a cut of pork with crackling is also a winner for this dish. Biksemad is full of flavor and yummy fats so you don't need a lot to fill you up and keep you going. We love this one for breakfast as well as dinner.

INGREDIENTS

- 1kg pork neck
- 1 cup bone broth
- 4 long rashers of streaky bacon
- 8 medium potatoes, par-boiled
- A good slug or two of olive oil
- Salt and pepper
- Tabasco, or similar hot sauce
- 2 green apples, cut into chunks
- Egg, to serve (optional)

METHOD

Put pork neck into a heavy based casserole dish and pour over bone broth. Pop a lid on top and place into the oven on 190°C for 2 hours or until soft and tender. Once cooled enough, chop the pork into bite sized chunks and put into a large oven tray with high sides. Cut bacon into similar sized pieces and add to pork. Add par-boiled potatoes to the porks. We like to smash the potatoes down very slightly before adding them in so that the increased surface area allows them to become crispy and golden.

Add a good few slugs of olive oil, some hot sauce and lots of salt and pepper to the mix. Place back into the oven for 30-40 minutes until potatoes start to color. Add apple and pop back in for another 5-10 minutes until it is soft and just cooked. Enjoy with lots of fresh salad and a heavy hand with Tabasco or a similar spicy sauce.

A fresh cracked egg straight into a steaming hot biksemad is the best way to enjoy it.

mel's meatballs

Meatballs are a solid weekly item on the menu at home. I love them because I can add so much nutrition to the meat, cook them in advance and just heat for dinner and serve with a salad when I am working late in the clinic. Adding spices changes the dynamic of a dish and adds loads of health benefits. Chermoula gives a mildly spicy Moroccan flavor to these meatballs with paprika, lemon and garlic tones. You can buy it pre-made from good spice shops.

INGREDIENTS

- 1kg grass fed beef mince
- 1 big handful of baby spinach, roughly chopped
- 1 large grated carrot
- 1 grated zucchini
- 1 large handful of basil, roughly chopped
- 3 cloves of garlic, smashed
- 1 teaspoon of chermoula spice mix
- Zest of 1 lemon
- 1 egg
- Salt and pepper

METHOD

Throw all the ingredients into a big bowl and get your hands into it. Once mixed well start to roll into medium sized balls. Rather than cook them off separately in a fry pan, which I find time consuming and messy, line them up in an oven tray and cook on 180°C for around 20 minutes. Once the meatballs are cooked they can be kept in the fridge for up to 3 days and reheated as desired.

Enjoy on spiraled vegetables or with fresh salad.

simple veggie stack

INGREDIENTS

- 3 zucchini
- 1 cauliflower
- ½ Japanese/kent pumpkin
- 2 capsicums
- 4 tablespoons savory yeast flakes
- 2 cans coconut cream
- 2 cups broth or stock
- 2 teaspoons of smoked paprika
- Salt and pepper

METHOD

Slice all vegetables thinly. I like to use a mandolin to do this but can just be done with a knife. Layer the veg like a lasagne into a baking tray. I like to do a layer of each veg and then repeat until you are 5 cm from the top. The size of the dish needed will depend on the amount of veg you have and how many you want to feed. I often do 2 baking trays worth as it is so popular.

Mix coconut cream and stock with paprika and yeast. Add a generous amount of salt and pepper here as well. Mix it up and pour over veg stacks until it covers the top. Cover with a tight fitting lid or foil and bake for 45 minutes at 180°C or until a knife goes in smoothly. If you would like to crisp up the top, take the cover off and leave in oven on 200°C for a further 10 mins.

supercharged koftas

I love a good kofta and anything that has mince means one thing-you can supercharge it by hiding loads of goodies in the mix and adding buckets of flavor. This is my easy, mid-week version of a kofta (no skewers here, sir) which can be made in advance, rolled and set aside for up to 48 hours before cooking. If your mince has been thawed, then best to cook immediately after rolling. They can be eaten hot or cold and make a great addition to the lunch box for adults and children alike as they are easy to handle. Serve with homemade hummus, quinoa salad and flatbread or simply fresh steamed veg.

INGREDIENTS

- 1kg lamb mince
- 1 carrot
- 1 onion
- 1 zucchini
- 1 small head broccoli, including stem
- 1 small capsicum, deseeded
- 2-3 chillies (optional and to taste)
- 2 small slices bread
- 2 eggs or 3 chia seed eggs
- 3 teaspoons cumin
- 1 teaspoon paprika
- 1 teaspoon salt
- Freshly cracked pepper

METHOD

Pop the mince into a large bowl and set aside.

Start to throw veggies into the food processor until finely diced and add to bowl with mince as ready. Add chilli if you like a little heat. Pop your slices of bread into the processor and whiz until fine. Add to bowl. Add eggs, spices and salt and pepper. Now get your hands dirty. There is no other way to do it. Mix the meat and veg together well. Start to roll handful size balls as pictured.

The easiest way to cook these guys is simply in the oven. You can fry them off if you want but I have found there is no need. Place in an oven tray without over crowding. Cook in a 180°C oven for 20-30 minutes until they are cooked through.

roast lamb with lemon & cumin

This is a staple in our house and something I can get ready in the morning and leave in the oven until I am ready to heat at night. It is simple and tasty, nutritious and full of protein and good fat. Cumin stimulates the pancreas helping you to digest your food better and therefore absorb more nutrients. It is also high in iron. While lemons are full of vitamin C, fighting cancer and boosting the immune system. Having slow cooked meat in the house is the perfect way to ensure you have food for lunches the next day, plus breakfast if you are like us and enjoy a hearty morning meal.

INGREDIENTS

- 2 kg lamb shoulder
- 4 fresh lemons, halved
- 3 heaped tablespoons cumin
- 1 teaspoon salt
- fresh cracked pepper
- 1 cup bone broth
- 1 cup preservative free red wine

METHOD

Place the lamb into an oven tray or a casserole dish if you have one big enough. Squeeze the juice from the lemons over the top and drop the lemons into the dish as well. Sprinkle the cumin, salt and pepper over the lamb and rub slightly to spread around. Add the bone broth and wine to the bottom of the pan.

If you are using an oven tray use some aluminum foil to cover the lamb well. If it is not covered well enough it may dry out. Either way, keep your eye on it throughout the day and add a little more broth if needed.

If you are using a casserole dish, simply pop the lid on. Place in the oven on 170°C for at least 5 hours. I will often pop this on in the morning and turn it off mid-afternoon, leaving it in the oven. I will then just turn the oven back on at 200°C to heat it through for 20 minutes at dinner time.

This lamb is great with pickled red onion (page 29) and a side of the roast beet and quinoa salad (page 134).

mel's veggie spaghetti with nutty citrus avo pesto

INGREDIENTS

- Zucchini, squash, carrot, or mixed spaghetti (use a spiralizer or a mandolin, or just slice into thin strips)
- 1 avocado, deseeded and peeled
- ¼ cup almonds
- 4 limes, juiced
- 2 tablespoons pepitas
- 1-2 cloves garlic
- ½ bunch basil, roughly chopped
- ½ bunch parsley, roughly chopped
- 2 tablespoons olive oil
- Grated macadamias, almonds or pine nuts, lime wedges, and basil for garnish

METHOD

In a food processor, blend together the avocado, almonds, lime juice, pepitas, garlic, basil, parsley, and olive oil. Cover the veggie spaghetti with all but a few tablespoons of the pesto.

Arrange the spaghetti and pesto mix into serving bowls.

Top it with a dollop of remaining pesto.
Garnish with some fresh basil leaves, macadamias, almonds or pine nuts, and some lime wedges.

butter chicken

This recipe is super easy and can usually get you through the first half of the week as dinner and then as lunches.

INGREDIENTS

- 1 onion, diced
- 6 cloves garlic
- 3 tablespoons turmeric powder
- 1 tablespoon each of spice powders – ginger, cardamom, coriander, cumin and paprika
- 1-1.5 kg chicken thighs, whole and untrimmed
- 2-3 cans coconut cream
- 1-2 cups homemade broth (see bone broth recipe on page 42)
- 1 can crushed tomatoes
- Salt & pepper
- Squeeze of lemon juice
- Pinch of chili flakes (optional)

METHOD

Sauté the onion and garlic in coconut oil in a big sturdy pot until cooked.

Add spices and cook for a few minutes, letting the aromas build. Add the chicken and coat it in the spices, stirring for a few minutes. Add in the coconut cream, some of the homemade stock, and tomatoes.

Put the lid on and leave to simmer for as long as you desire, stirring occasionally to avoid burning the bottom. You can also transfer the pot to the oven at this stage to avoid a burnt bottom and cook on low for 2-3 hours.

You can also add veggies in with 10 minutes left to go and stir. I suggest kale, broccoli and beans.

Squeeze with lemon and season with salt & pepper before serving.
This can be served with cauliflower rice (see page 221 for recipe).
Enjoy!

sweet salmon patties

INGREDIENTS

- 2 cups sweet potato (or half sweet potato & half white)
- 2 tablespoons coconut flour
- 2 tablespoons cumin
- 1 tablespoon paprika
- 2 eggs (or chia seed eggs)
- 1 large can of good quality salmon
- 1 cup english spinach, washed well & set aside to dry
- 1 carrot, grated
- 2 lemons
- salt & pepper
- 2 teaspoons sesame seeds
- Olive oil or coconut oil, for frying
- 2 tablespoons fresh dill, stems removed (optional)

METHOD

When buying canned salmon, look for BPA free cans from your local healthood store and companies that catch their fish with integrity.

Steam potatoes until a knife sticks into them easily. Try not to over cook to maintain as much nutrients as possible. Strain and keep the cooking water. Mash the potato in a large bowl and allow it to cool. Add the coconut flour, spices, eggs, and salmon. Chop the spinach roughly and add this in with the carrot and the juice and zest of one lemon. Salt and pepper to taste, throw the sesame seeds in and give it all a good stir to bring together.

Start to use your hands to bring the mixture together and form medium size balls. If the mixture is too dry use a little of your cooking water until you can form moist and strong balls. If it is too wet sprinkle a little more coconut our over the mix.

Put a few tablespoons of oil in a fry pan and heat to medium. Start to cook the salmon patties in small batches, pressing down to flatten them before turning. Pop them in the oven to keep warm while cooking all the patties.

Garnish with sliced lemon. Serve with fresh salad and chili.

I like to stack the patties over a pile of salad and make a simple dressing of 2 tablespoons white wine vinegar, 2-3 tablespoons warm water, ½ teaspoon coconut sugar, salt and pepper and fresh cut chili to drizzle over the top.

lamb korma

This dish is well worth the effort with all the herbs and spices. It is great for leftovers and it a healthy version of a take-away favourite. Enjoy on its own or with cauliflower rice.

INGREDIENTS

- 3 tablespoons garam masala (can buy pre-made from a good quality spice shop)
- 8 cardamom pods, bruised
- 5 cloves, whole
- 1 tablespoon coriander seeds
- 2 teaspoons cumin seeds
- 1 pinch saffron threads
- 2 tablespoons coconut oil or ghee
- 1kg boneless lamb shoulder, cut into chunks or slow cooked whole as I do when I have the time (pictured)
- Sea salt & fresh cracked pepper
- 1 onion, finely chopped
- 1 cup bone broth (see page 42 for recipe)
- 2 cans coconut cream
- ½ cup cashews, ground
- 1 cinnamon stick
- ¼ teaspoon ground turmeric

METHOD

Start with a large heavy based pot. There is no need to use multiple pans. Lightly dry fry your garam marsala until it smells fragrant, then add in the cardamom and cloves. Heat for 1 minute. Shake the pan and add the coriander and cumin seeds for a further minute. Set aside.

Put the saffron in a small bowl and cover with 2 tablespoons of cold water. Set aside and let it soak for at least 10 minutes.

Melt 1 tablespoon of the coconut oil or ghee in a large saucepan over medium heat and season the lamb with salt & pepper. When the oil or ghee is hot but not smoking, add the lamb in batches and brown for 1-2 minutes on each side. Once the lamb is browned on all sides, transfer to a plate.

Add the remaining oil or ghee to the pan, along with the onion, reduce the heat to medium-low, and cook, stirring for 5 minutes. Add the garam masala spices and mix well. Return the lamb to the pan with any juices that have accumulated on the plate.

Stir well to coat the lamb with the spices. Add the stock, coconut milk, ground cashews, cinnamon, saffron with its soaking water, turmeric and bring to a low simmer. Cover and cook over a low heat for 2-3 hours, stirring and ensuring it doesn't burn on the bottom. You could also pop it in the oven at this stage for 1-2 hours instead of leaving it on the cooktop if you prefer.

Uncover, stir, and if necessary, cook uncovered until the sauce is reduced and thick. Season with additional salt & pepper and serve.

If you wish to slow cook whole simply brown the lamb on all sides as pictured and place into a slow cooker. Follow the instructions for the sauce as above, skipping the addition of the lamb and add the finished product to the slow cooker. Leave on low for the day.

cauliflower fried rice

If you don't have these veggies, just use whatever is in the fridge. This is a versatile leftovers dish.

INGREDIENTS

- 1 cauliflower, chopped roughly into small pieces
- 1 corn on the cob
- 4 free-range bacon rashers, diced
- 2 eggs, whisked (optional)
- 2 tablespoons coconut oil
- 1 onion, finely chopped
- 1 carrot, diced
- 2 garlic cloves, finely chopped
- ½ red capsicum, diced
- ½ yellow capsicum, diced
- 2 cm ginger, peeled & finely grated
- 2 tablespoons tamari
- Handful of kale, roughly chopped

METHOD

You can throw your cauliflower into a food processor if you like. I find it easy to just chop it up into bite sized pieces as it breaks apart while cooking.

Pop your corn cob (whole) into a frypan with some coconut oil and let it cook, turning it often while you prep the rest. Fry the bacon and set aside. Mix the eggs in a bowl and cook like an omelette. Set aside and cut into strips when cooled.

Heat the coconut oil in the pan over high heat, add the onion, carrot, and garlic and cook for a few minutes. Stir in the capsicum and ginger and cook for another few minutes. Add the cauliflower and cook for 2-3 minutes, or until tender. Add in the bacon, egg, tamari, and kale and cook for 2 minutes, or until everything is heated through and well combined.

Cut your corn off the cob and add it to the dish or serve it on the side.
Garnish with some chili flakes if you like it hot.

one pot sausage & veg

An effortless, colorful, and healthy way to warm up on a cold night.

INGREDIENTS

- Olive oil
- 12 good quality pork, beef or veggie sausages
- 1 red onion, chopped
- 1 head & stem of broccoli, chopped
- 2 cups pumpkin, chopped
- 1 zucchini, sliced
- 2 carrots, chopped roughly
- 1 cup mushrooms
- 1 can tomatoes
- 1 tablespoon cumin
- 1 tablespoon paprika
- 2 cups bone broth (see page 42)

METHOD

Throw all of your ingredients except broccoli and mushrooms into a hard-based casserole dish and pop in the oven at 180° C for 2 hours.

Throw in the broccoli and mushrooms with 5 minutes to go.

This stew is great served with the sweet tatie mash (see page 121).

Chapter 10
SWEET NOTHINGS

nana's no fail banana slice

Through food we can communicate how we feel. We can show love and that we care. Food has always been turned to in times of pain, grief, loss, happiness and celebration. It is these emotions that we are sharing we when we cook and share food. It is these emotions that created this book. This slice was one of the first of my taste memories and it transports me every time I smell it baking in the oven. I have adapted it over the years to make it healthier, gluten free and dairy free whilst still preserving its essence. I cooked it recently for my Nana who created it and she could barely notice the difference.

INGREDIENTS

- 1 ½ cups gluten free self raising flour or spelt flour
- ½ cup radpadura or coconut sugar
- ¼ teaspoon bi-carb soda (look for aluminum free)
- ½ teaspoon of good quality cinnamon powder (don't let spices get old and sit in the pantry for years)
- ½ teaspoon good quality nutmeg powder
- 125g grass fed butter
- ¼ cup macadamia milk (or your choice – almond, coconut, dairy)
- 2-3 ripe bananas, mashed
- 1 egg
- A good pinch of salt

METHOD

Preheat oven to 180° C and line a small slice tin.

Place all the dry ingredients into a large bowl and stir to combine. Melt the butter in a small saucepan on low until just liquid- do not over heat or let it boil. Set aside to cool slightly.

Add milk, bananas, egg and salt to dry ingredients and mix. Add butter and stir for just a few minutes until the mix has come together. Do not over mix.

Cook in the oven for around 45 minutes or until the cake is firm to touch.

Play around with add-ins such as nuts to give it a crunch, or top it whole banana slices for some texture.

peanut butter cacao cups

These little guys are packed full of good fats. Macadamias in particular contain monounsaturated fats and omega, meaning they are high in antioxidants and help reduce the risk of heart disease. When it comes down to it, this is the type of dessert that gives back, giving you that delicious sweet hit but not spiking your blood sugar levels.

INGREDIENTS

For the base:
- 1 cup macadamias
- 1 cup cashews
- 2 large tablespoons of 100% natural peanut butter
- 5 medjool dates (pitted) or 10 small organic apricots
- 1 tablespoon cacao nibs
- 2 tablespoons hemp seeds
- 2 teaspoons honey or maple syrup (optional)
- 3 teaspoons Amazonia Spiced Cacao Powder (optional)
- Pinch of salt
- ½ cup shredded coconut flakes

For the top:
- 1 block of Loving Earth chocolate (or other plain organic dark choc)
- Cacao nibs to decorate

METHOD

Pop all ingredients for the base into a food processor except water and coconut flakes. Blend until it comes together like a dough. If it gets stuck or looks dry add a teaspoon of water at a time until it comes together.

Use a small cupcake tray or whatever shape you would like. Sprinkle some coconut into each of the mold so that your fudge does not stick. Press the mix into the molds firmly.

Top with melted chocolate and cacao nibs and place in the fridge to set.

beetroot cupcakes

INGREDIENTS

- 2 large beetroots, washed & grated raw
- 2 eggs (or chia eggs)
- ½ teaspoon vanilla powder
- 1 teaspoon cinnamon
- Pinch of sea salt
- 1 ½ cup almond meal
- 4 tablespoons raw cacao powder
- 3 tablespoons coconut oil
- ¼ cup honey or maple syrup

METHOD

Preheat the oven to 170°C and line a cupcake tin with 12 cupcake cases.

Blend all the ingredients together using a blender or a stick blender until it's a smooth batter. Divide the batter between the 12 cases. Bake for 40 minutes.

OPTIONAL

Ice the cupcakes using some whipped coconut cream (see page 244) and top with a sprinkle of vanilla bean powder or any other topping of your choice. Yum!

cashew butter bar

A quick and easy muesli bar to prepare for the week to come. Perfect for a mid-afternoon snack or lunchboxes. You can easily make it nut free for school by using sunflower seed butter instead of cashew butter and just using 2 cups of seeds and dried fruit.

INGREDIENTS

- ½ cup cashew butter
- ½ cup butter
- ¼ cup honey or maple syrup
- 2 cups mixed nuts, seeds, dried fruit of your choice

METHOD

Line a small oven tray or glass dish with baking paper.

Melt the cashew butter, butter and honey until just coming together. Take off the heat to cool slightly.

Place your mix of selected nuts and seeds into a large bowl and coat with the nutty butter mix well. Pour into lined tray and press down firmly into a bar. The tray you use will determine the thickness of your bar.

Pop in the fridge to set for at least 2 hours.

When ready, slice into small bars for school or work or just as a healthy treat at home.
Will last 1 week in the fridge (if you hide it!).

Note: You may need more or less nuts and seeds depending on the density of those you use. The mix should be wet and everything well coated, not drowned. Just add more dry ingredients if it is looking too wet.

cacao & coffee raw cheesecake

INGREDIENTS

For the base:
- 1 ½ cups hazelnuts (or swap for sunflower seeds for nut free)
- 4 medjool dates (fresh and pitted or if dried just soaked for 10 mins prior in warm water)
- 1 large pinch pink salt
- 2 tablespoons raw cacao powder
- 1 tablespoon un-hulled tahini
- ¼ cup coconut flakes

For the filling:
- 1 cup macadamias (swap for sunflower seeds for nut free)
- 1 cup hemp seeds
- 1 cup pepitas
- ¾ cup honey or maple syrup
- 2 tablespoons coffee beans
- ¼ cup coconut oil
- ½ cup coconut cream

For the topping:
- 2 cups raw cashews (sunflower seeds if you want nut free)
- 1 banana
- 1 shot of coffee or 2 teaspoons instant in 1 tablespoon water
- 4 dates, pitted
- 1 ½ cups almond milk
- ⅓ cup coconut oil
- Seeds from 1 vanilla pod
- 1 teaspoon cinnamon
- Pinch of salt

To decorate:
cacao nibs, dark chocolate coated coffee beans, buckinis, goji berries, pepitas, whole hazelnuts or whatever else you like.

METHOD

Use a food processor or Thermie to bring all ingredients from the base together, except the coconut flakes.

Use a spring-loaded tin for ease in removing after set. Sprinkle the coconut flakes on the bottom of your tin as the first layer and to help prevent the cake sticking. Press the base mixture down into the pan to form the crust. Place in freezer while making the filling. Blend all the filling ingredients in a food processor. No need to wash in between. Pour mixture on top of crust and return to the freezer.

Next, process all ingredients for the top layer until very smooth. Pour this mixture on top of the cake. Now comes the fun part! Decorate your cake with an array of treats such as chocolate coated coffee beans. Place the cake back in freezer for 4-5 hours. Add edible flowers if you want to impress, after you remove from freezer.

Pull the cake out of the freezer about 10 minutes before you want to slice and serve.

strawberries & cream raw cheesecake

INGREDIENTS

For the crust:
- 1½ cups macadamia nuts (or swap ½ for walnuts)
- ½ cup medjool dates (fresh and depitted or if dried just soaked for 10 mins prior in warm water)
- ¼ cup coconut flakes
- 1 large pinch pink salt

For the filling:
- 2½ cups cashews
- ¾ cup lemon juice
- ½-¾ cup maple syrup (depending how sweet you like it)
- ¾ cup coconut oil
- The seeds of 1 scraped vanilla pod
- ¼ cup water, if needed to assist blending (optional)

For the topping:
- 2 cups organic frozen mixed berries
- ½ cup dates
- 270g can of coconut cream
- Handful of cacao nibs and fruit to decorate the top (optional)

METHOD

Use a food processor or Thermie to break down macadamia nuts, salt and dates until mostly smooth but not too dense. Use a spring-loaded tin for ease in removing after set. Sprinkle the coconut flakes on the bottom of your tin as the first layer and to help prevent the cake sticking. Press the macadamia and date mixture down into the pan to form the crust. Place in freezer while making the filling.

Blend all the filling ingredients in a food processor. A little water can be added to help process the ingredients. Pour mixture on top of crust. Place the cake back in the freezer for an hour to firm up.

After this, process the frozen mixed berries, dates and coconut cream until very smooth. I don't bother washing the blender between layers-a little mix up is fine. Blend until nice and smooth. Pour this mixture on top of the cheesecake and sprinkle with cacao nibs or whatever topping your heart desires. You may also try shaved Loving Earth or Pana Choc as a topping, add some fruit or leave it plain. Place the cheesecake back in freezer for about 4-5 hours.

Slice cheesecake while frozen and let sit for about 15-20 minutes before serving.

Part 3

Homemade Staples

LSA

LSA is a blend of ground linseeds (flax seeds), sunflower seeds, and almonds. It is important that the flaxseeds are ground, as whole flaxseeds cannot be broken down well by the body. This mix is an amazing source of dietary fiber, protein, omega fatty acids, minerals, and vitamins.

INGREDIENTS

- ¾ cup raw flaxseeds
- ½ cup raw sunflower seeds
- ¼ cup raw almonds

METHOD

Pop all of the ingredients into a food processor and blend it into a fine meal. Store in an air-tight container. Add into smoothies for extra nutrient goodness, or use in baking, such as bread.

---

chia seed eggs

A chia seed egg makes the perfect egg substitute for whatever you're cooking, from vegan baking, to binding veggie burgers, or for those with egg allergies. They are full of fantastic nutrients, such as fiber, protein and omega 3 fatty acids. They are also gluten-free, grain-free and an excellent source of vitamins and minerals. If you don't want the chia seeds to be visible in your cooking, just use white chia seeds as opposed to black ones.

INGREDIENTS

- 1 tablespoon chia seeds
- 3 tablespoons water

METHOD

Mix the chia seeds with the water and let set for 5-15 minutes, or until the water is all soaked up and it has developed a goopy texture similar to raw eggs. Use in place of 1 egg. Double if the recipe calls for more than one egg, however it will not work in recipes with over 3 eggs.

tomato base sauce

INGREDIENTS

- 2 onions, chopped finely
- 4 tablespoons olive oil
- 6 cloves of garlic, smashed & chopped finely
- 2 kg of mixed tomatoes (roma, truss, cherry, egg or variations you like) chopped
- ½ cup preservative free red wine (or broth)
- 1 tablespoon of brown sugar (Tomatoes need sugar! You can use an alternative like maple syrup but start with 1 teaspoon & taste as you go)
- 4-5 sprigs of fresh thyme
- 2 tablespoons dried oregano
- 1 teaspoon salt
- Fresh cracked pepper

METHOD

Place onions and oil into a large heavy based casserole dish, over a low-medium heat. Sweat onions down by stirring over the heat for around 10 minutes. Do not let them brown, we want them juicy, succulent and see through rather than crispy and blackened. Turn the heat right down and give them more time if they need. Once they are there add the garlic and give it five minutes, stirring. Turn the heat up to high and add the tomatoes, stirring. Let them get hot and start to bubble, break down and stick to the bottom (just a tad) for around 10 minutes depending on your heat.
Once things are getting hot, add the wine to bring all those beautiful bits away from the bottom of the pot and stir through. Add the sugar, herbs, salt and pepper and stir well. Turn the sauce down to a simmer and pop the lid on. Check it in 10 minutes just to make sure the bottom does not burn and let it sit on low for around 1 hour. Then, remove the lid and let it simmer with it off for 20 minutes until it thickens slightly.

---

cauliflower rice

Great for lunch the next day or pair with your favorite curry for a heartier meal.

INGREDIENTS

- 1 head organic cauliflower including the stem
- Salt & Pepper
- Coconut oil
- Spices for seasoning such as garlic, turmeric, or chili flakes (optional)

METHOD

Roughly chop up the cauliflower and throw it into a food processor. Blitz until fine.

Heat coconut oil in a large frying pan and add in the cauliflower and your choice of spices. Cook for 10-15 minutes per batch or until cauliflower is soft and slightly browned. You may need to do this in a few batches depending on how much cauliflower you have.

Serve as you would rice.

whipped coconut cream

Use as an alternative for frosting on things like cupcakes.

INGREDIENTS

- 1 can full fat coconut cream, cold
- 1 vanilla bean
- dash of maple syrup

METHOD

Refrigerate a can of full fat coconut cream overnight, or just keep one in the fridge at all times in case of a need for cream. Scoop out the solids and leave the liquid. Place in a bowl or a Mixmaster for whipping.

Whip for 5-6 minutes, or until it starts to thicken. Add the seeds from the inside of the vanilla pod, and a dash of maple syrup. Whip for a further 2-3 minutes until stiff peaks form.

Enjoy!

---

ranch dressing

Will make any boring green salad into a superstar.

INGREDIENTS

- 1 avocado, mashed
- 2 tablespoons coconut oil
- 2 tablespoons coconut cream
- 1 tablespoon apple cider vinegar
- 1 tablespoon parsley
- 1 teaspoon wholegrain mustard

METHOD

To make the ranch dressing, mix together the avocado, coconut oil, coconut cream, vinegar, parsley, mustard, and a pinch of salt and pepper to taste.

homemade mayo

INGREDIENTS

- 1 egg, room temperature
- Pinch of salt
- Pinch of pepper
- 1 teaspoon of apple cider vinegar
- 1 teaspoon Dijon mustard
- 1 cup of oil – I recommend grapeseed oil as it is mild. You could also use half grapeseed, half olive oil for a more fruity and robust flavor

METHOD

Crack the egg into a bowl (if using a hand blender) or the bowl of food processor. Add all other ingredients except oil. Give this a quick whiz for 30 seconds. Now start to add oil. Start with just a teaspoon. Whiz for 30 seconds. Another teaspoon and so on until the mix becomes a little thicker. Now, start to pour oil in a slow drizzle while whizzing at the same time until all the oil is gone. There you have it – easy, no-fail, super tasty, additive-free mayo!
Mix it up by adding different flavours to your mayo.

Chermoula Sauce
Chermoula is a Moroccan spice blend which adds zest and kick to any meat or veg dish. It also makes a spicy sauce when mixed with your homemade mayo. To 1 cup homemade mayo just add 2 tablespoons chermoula spice mix, ½ cup fresh lemon juice and 2 tablespoons hot sauce, like tabasco and stir.

Pomegranate Mayo
Use a wooden spoon to knock the seeds and juice of half a pomegranate into 1 cup of homemade mayo. Add 1 teaspoon of pomegranate molasses and stir.

MEL'S HINTS FOR HEALTHY COOKING

A QUICK GUIDE TO SUGAR

1 cup sugar = 1 teaspoon liquid stevia
1 tbsp sugar = 6-9 drops liquid stevia
1 teaspoon sugar = 2-4 drops liquid stevia

White sugar can be replaced by granulated stevia, xylitol, dextrose/glucose, coconut sugar, or rapadura using a 1:1 ratio. In recipes that call for liquid sweeteners, rice malt syrup, honey, maple syrup, and agave are interchangeable.

Some helpful hints when using different sugars:

- Xylitol will not be as sweet but you tend to get used to it quickly. It can be used in place of sugar in any recipe that doesn't require the sugar to break down into liquid form—it is impossible for xylitol to caramelize even at an extremely high temperature or when cooked at length.

- Dextrose needs extra wet ingredients, so you can add an extra egg. Make sure to not over-beat it, and to not let it burn.

- Coconut sugar and rapadura are great for replacing brown sugar as they have a stronger flavor and a caramel color and texture. They can be over powering in light baking, such as a sponge cake, but work great for banana bread or sticky date pudding.

- Honey will give a honey taste as well as the sweetness.

- Rice malt syrup will just add sweetness.

- Agave can come in light, dark, and raw. The darker the color, the more caramel-like the flavor will be. Light agave just adds sweetness.

- When using natural sweeteners, remember to always keep the end product in the fridge and don't keep for too long as sugar is a preservative but these are not.

A QUICK GUIDE TO OILS

When using oil, there are a few options with slight differences:

- Coconut oil and ghee are great for high heat cooking.
- Extra virgin olive oil has a stronger flavor and lower smoke point, making it good for dressings, marinades, sauces and low-heat cooking.
- Avocado oil is lightly flavored, and carries other flavors well. It has a very high smoke point.
- Nut oils (almond, hazelnut, macadamia, peanut, pecan, walnut) are great but only certain nut oils can be used for cooking. Macadamia and peanut, for example, have high smoke points, but walnut oil should only be used in dressings.

IN-THE-KITCHEN RECOMMENDATIONS

- Use organic wherever possible
- Use organic free-range eggs if available
- Keep skin on vegetables
- Use activated nuts and seeds
- Use filtered water where possible
- Use non-iodized salts such as Himalayan or Celtic sea salt
- These are foolproof recipes, so don't worry about over chopping or specially slicing everything
- These recipes are family sized meals unless otherwise noted

When using vanilla, try to always use whole vanilla beans. When buying, look for plump beans that look glossy on the outside and bend a little when you touch them. Beans that are dull looking and brittle are hard to scrape seeds from. 1 vanilla bean = about 3 teaspoons vanilla extract.

HEALTHY CONDIMENT OPTIONS

- Bragg's herbal sprinkle
- coconut aminos
- red/white wine vinegar
- Bragg's healthy vinaigrette
- organic Dijon mustard
- seaweed flakes
- Himalayan crystal salt
- organic cold pressed olive oil
- organic pepper
- any fresh herbs
- mashed avo + coconut cream makes a nice ranch dressing
- organic nothing added coconut cream/milk
- organic unhulled tahini

THE MGHERBS ONE WEEK DETOX

A detox should not be a quick weight loss fix, but a method to prepare the ground (your body) for long term harvest. A comprehensive detoxification program should be a means to achieve your goals, yes. But, also and most importantly, to set up long term sustainable lifestyle changes to achieve fundamental improvements in your health. Now and in the future. Our body will give us back what we put in. So, what are you putting in yours?

Toxicity is unavoidable in today's modern society. When we walk outside we are exposed via our lungs, skin, and digestive system. Toxins are in our air, food, water and soil.

There are exotoxins (outside factors) which include alcohol, nicotine, car fumes, industrial waste, pesticides, herbicides, food additives including colorings and flavorings, pharmaceuticals, recreational drugs, solvents and heavy metals. There are also endogenous (inside factors) toxins. These are by-products from metabolism and impaired digestion.

Toxins from within emphasize the importance of a healthy gut flora as many toxic metabolites and by products are the result of dysbiosis. The imbalance of good and bad bacteria in your gut. When foods are not digested properly they become fuel for harmful or pathogenic bacteria and yeasts. As the bad guys grow and reproduce the good guys get pushed out of the way and die off. The terms dysbiosis and leaky gut have been related to diseases as varied as depression, chronic fatigue syndrome, autism and autoimmunity.

So where do we start? The first and easiest thing that we can do is reduce the burden on our body. We do this by reducing as much of our toxic load as possible through healthy diet and lifestyle choices. As well daily choices about what you put in your hair and on your skin, even what you brush your teeth with. Perfumes, makeup, deodorants are often toxic and there are natural alternatives.

The second is to enhance the body's natural detoxification capacity. This can be done by cleaning up gut function and reducing the production of internal toxins. We can do all of this and improve the function of the liver and kidney excretory channels with food.

Here, I have created an easy one week meal planner to show you how easy it is to eat healthy and utilize the recipes from this book, while detoxing at the same time. This type of meal planning is also safe and versatile for the whole family and to do long term if you chose. I call it meal planning rather than diet as it will hopefully help shift your food habits for the better and become the norm, rather than a short-term diet. Remember, all whole and real foods are medicine to our body.

TIPS FOR GETTING STARTED

- Highlight your options for the week & what day you will consume them.

- Use at least 3 different options for each individual meal during your week (e.g. 3 different breakfast choices, 3 different lunch choices etc).

- Vegetables on the meal planner can be used for breakfast or lunch.

- Feel free to exclude those foods you do not like but do not add any which don't feature on the meal planner.

- Enjoy 2-3 snacks per day as well as breakfast, lunch & dinner, depending on your energy requirements-this is how hungry you are on a day to day basis.

- Eat organic & free-range wherever possible.

- The key to sticking to the meal planner is organization. Use your shopping list & have all the foods you need available at home.

- Plan your meals & have them ready the day/night before.

- Enjoy as much water, coconut water (check for added ingredients), detox tea, or other herbal teas as you wish

- Make smoothie cubes. Make your smoothies in advance, freeze them in ice cubes, and just whizz up with extra liquid when you want one.

SHOPPING LIST

Veggies
Kale or Spinach
Cabbage
Shallots
Onions
Bok Choy
Asparagus
Sauerkraut of any kind (avoid added sugar, colors and preservative. Only buy from fridge as shelf products are pasteurized)
Baby spinach (lots.)
2 Avocados
Celery
Fennel bulb
2 Cucumbers
Garlic
Beetroots
Carrots
Red onion
Broccoli
Radish
Rocket
Snow Peas
Grated carrot or beetroot or zucchini or squash
Cauliflower

Fruit
6 Lemons
Bunch of bananas
5 Green apples
1 Pear
Berries of your choice
Paw paw
Watermelon
1 Orange

Non-Dairy
Almond milk
Coconut water

Frozen
Mixed berries or gojis
2 frozen bananas (peel before freezing)

Proteins
Eggs
Can tuna
1 Can chickpeas
Tuna
Chicken
Salmon
Eggs
Lentils or legumes
Black beans/adzuki/lima/chickpeas 500g
Organic chicken livers

Carbohydrates
Almond meal
Coconut flour
Quinoa crackers
Brown rice
Quinoa
Basmati rice
Lentils
Butter beans
Kidney beans
Yellow split peas
Black beans
Zucchini or carrot spaghetti
Black bean pasta
Kelp noodles
Cauliflower rice (see recipe page 243)
Millet
Buckwheat

Seasonings
Himalayan sea salt
Cinnamon powder
Honey
Ginger powder
Cumin
Fresh thyme

Nuts & Seeds
Walnuts
Chia seeds
Choice of nuts/seeds for the Crunchy Nutty No Grainola
Sesame seeds
Almonds
Cashews
Brazil Nuts
Sunflower seeds
Pumpkin seeds
LSA (see tips page 240)

Other Pantry Items
Coconut oil
Coconut flakes
Bicarbonate of Soda
Raw apple cider vinegar
Tahini paste
Dried apricots
Natural peanut butter or other nut butter
Olive oil

Optional Additions
Raw Amazonian Protein Powder

BREAKFAST

Start each day with a squeeze of lemon or a dash of Bragg's apple cider vinegar in warm water.

DAY 1
Green Omelette (see page 163).

DAY 2
½ cup Crunchy Nutty No Grain-ola (see page 171) with almond milk, chopped banana, and berries or try with ½ cup coconut yoghurt.

DAY 3
Detox Smoothie (see page 104).

DAY 4
2 slices of Nutty Seedy Bread (see page 152) spread with avocado oil and topped with 1 full avocado & a squeeze of lemon and a sprinkle of Himalayan salt.

DAY 5
Alkalizing Smoothie (see page 109).

DAY 6
2 slices of Nutty Seedy bread (see page 152), spread with coconut oil, topped with 1-2 chopped bananas, handful of walnuts, ½ teaspoon cinnamon powder, ½ teaspoon honey, & 1 tablespoon chia seeds.

DAY 7
Chia pudding (see page 168).

LUNCH

Highlight your lunch choices on your shopping list.

PICK A BASE

Start with at least 1-1.5 cups of any or a mix of the following

- Beetroots
- Carrots
- Red onion
- Cabbage
- Radish
- Grated carrot, beetroot, zucchini, and/or squash
- Sauerkraut (avoid sugars, colors & preservatives. Only buy from fridge as shelf products are pasteurized)
- Baby spinach
- Rocket
- Snow peas
- Avocado
- Broccoli (raw)

ADD A PROTEIN

- 1-2 boiled eggs (if you didn't have any for breakfast)
- ½ cup lentils or legumes
- ½ cup black beans/lima/chickpeas
- 1 medium sized can tuna in olive oil
- 1 cup poached or stir-fried chicken
- 1 medium fillet of salmon or a medium size tin of salmon in olive oil

Enjoy any of the condiments from page 250 on your detox.

DINNER

Easy as 1, 2, 3...

Highlight the dinner choices on your shopping list and add to it if necessary.

CHOOSE A PALM SIZE SERVING OF PROTEIN

- Turkey
- Chicken
- Lamb
- Fishperch, whiting, salmon, barramundi, snapper
- Duck
- Kangaroo
- Black beans
- Legumes/lentils/beans

CHOOSE ¾ CUP OF A CARBOHYDRATE

- Brown rice
- Quinoa
- Basmati rice
- Lentils
- Butter beans
- Kidney beans
- Cauliflower rice
- Millet
- Buckwheat
- Yellow split peas
- Black beans
- Zucchini or carrot spaghetti (mandolin, veg pasta maker, slice thinly)
- Black bean pasta
- Kelp noodles

ADD AT LEAST 1 CUP OF VEGETABLES

- Cauliflower
- Broccoli
- Kale
- Spinach
- Cabbage
- Garlic
- Shallots
- Onions
- Bok Choy
- Asparagus
- Avocado
- Sauerkraut of any kind (avoid added sugar, colors, and preservatives. Only buy from fridge as shelf products have been pasteurized)

ACKNOWLEDGEMENTS

There are so many people that made this book possible.

Firstly, my clients. There is no greater pleasure or reward than what I am blessed to do for a job each day. To give people the tools and education to take their health into their own hands is an honor. I am so grateful for your trust in me. Without it, I would not be able to share my passion for food, natural medicine and holistic living. This book is for you and I hope that it gives you as much pleasure as it has given me to write, and that you can use it to break bread with your family and friends.

To Sara. My friend and unpaid worker bee. Thank you. Thank you. Thank you. I know that you are key to any success I have achieved now and in the future. Without you I would be lost and lonely. There would also be no photos for this book as I could not have prepped and cooked all of the food on my own!

Thank you to my family. Ever supportive and always with a table of plenty. I am so blessed to have been surrounded by great kitchen lovers, past and present, and I would not be who I am or find such joy in food without your influence and generosity.

Lastly, but just as importantly thank you to my beautiful, gentle and hungry husband and the little baby girl we have brought into the world. You inspire me every day and your support is ever lasting and without fail. I am humbled by your gracious presence and blessed by our shared passions for food and health. You allow me to be me. You are my rock, my home and my guinea pig. I am ever excited to feed our daughter with all of the love and food we have to offer and bring her into a world where she can appreciate what is on her plate and know where it has come from.

INDEX

ALKALISING SMOOTHIE	109
A MORNING BROTHEE	49
ANCHOVY MUSHROOMS	130
ASIAN POACHED CHICKEN	58
BEEF & HEART PIE	78
BEEF CHEEK STEW	57
BEETROOT CUPCAKES	230
BEETROOT HUMMUS	129
BLACK BREAKFAST	75
BONE BROTH	42
BREAK-FAST MUFFINS	176
BRISKET	54
BROTH BREKKIE	46
BUDDHA BOWL	184
BUG KILLER SMOOTHIE	104
BUTTER CHICKEN	214
CACAO & COFFEE RAW CHEESECAKE	234
CAPSICUM SALAD	118
CARAMEL SMOOTHIE	112
CASHEW BUTTER BAR	233
CASHEW CHEESE	141
CASHEW CREAM	141
CAULIFLOWER FRIED RICE	221
CAULIFLOWER RICE	243
CHIA PUDDING	168
CHIA SEED EGGS	240
CHICKEN BROTH	45
CHICKEN NUGGETS	192
CHOCOLATE GRANOLA	172
COCONUT PANCAKES	179
COCONUT PANNA COTTA	97
COLD TRIPE SALAD	67
CREAMY CUSTARD	93
CRUNCHY NUTTY NO GRAIN-OLA	171
CULTURED BEETS	13
CULTURED CARROT	10
DETOX SMOOTHIE	104
DETOX SOUP	183
DRINKING YOGHURT	94
FROSTY FRUIT BLOCKS	86
GLAMPING EGGS	175
GRANDAD'S LAMB FRY	64
GREEN OMELETTE	163
GUT GOLD SMOOTHIE	103
HEALTHY COLESLAW WITH POMEGRANATE DRESSING	137
HEALTHY SNICKERS SMOOTHIE	112
HOMEMADE MARSHMALLOWS	90
HOMEMADE MAYO	246
HOMEMADE PÂTÉ	71
JAPANESE GINGER PICKLE	30
JELLIES FOR THE LITTLES	82
KALE, QUINOA & ROAST VEG SALAD	191
KEFIR WATER	14
KIMCHI	6
KOMBUCHA	16
LAMB BRAINS	72
LAMB KORMA	218
LEFTOVER HASH	167
LEMON & DOUBLE MACA BALLS	148
LEMON & FENNEL SALAD	138
LSA	240
MEL'S CHICKEN & AVO SALAD WITH HOMEMADE RANCH DRESSING	195
MEL'S CLASSIC HUMMUS	122
MEL'S MEATBALLS	205
MEL'S VEGGIE SPAGHETTI WITH NUTTY CITRUS AVO PESTO	213
MISOMITE	9
NANA'S NO FAIL BANANA SLICE	226
NANA'S STEAK & KIDNEY PIE	76
NUTTY SEEDY LIFE CHANGING BREAD	152

ONE POT SAUSAGE & VEG	222
ORANGE, THYME & FIG PRESSURE COOKED CHICKEN	61
PALEO SNACK MIX	143
PEANUT BUTTER CACAO CUPS	229
PICKLED CARROTS	26
PICKLED GARLIC	34
PICKLED JALAPEÑOS	22
PICKLED RED ONION	29
PICKLING BRINE	21
PINEAPPLE LOLLIES	85
POTATO SALAD WITH OLIVES & MISO DRESSING	188
PRESSURE PORK BELLY	53
PUMPKIN & SPINACH FRITTATA	197
PUMPKIN SOUP	198
PURPLE PEOPLE EATER	110
QUICK CUCUMBER PICKLE	25
QUICK PICKLED MUSHROOMS	33
QUINOA TABBOULEH	133
RANCH DRESSING	244
ROAST BEET & QUINOA SALAD	134
ROAST LAMB WITH LEMON & CUMIN	210
RUSTIC SOURDOUGH BREAD	156
SAMMY'S BIKSEMAD	202
SAUERKRAUT	5
SCRUMMY SNACK MUFFINS	144
SEED BALLS	147
SHORT RIBS	50
SIMPLE VEGGIE STACK	206
SMOOTHIE CUBES	100
SNACK SMOOTHIE	110
SOURDOUGH STARTER	154
STRAWBERRIES & CREAM RAW CHEESECAKE	237
SUN-DRIED TOMATO & MINT HUMMUS	126
SUPERCHARGED KOFTAS	209
SWEET SALMON PATTIES	217
SWEET TATIE MASH	121
THE PERFECT PADDLE POP	89
THE ULTIMATE SMOOTHIE	107
TOMATO & MUSHROOM FOLDOVER	164
TOMATO BASE SAUCE	243
TUMERIC HUMMUS	125
TUMERIC LATTE	114
WARM TRIPE STEW	68
WEED SALAD WITH CITRUS SEGMENTS	187
WHIPPED COCONUT CREAM	244

www.ingramcontent.com/pod-product-compliance
Lightning Source LLC
Chambersburg PA
CBHW051401070526
44584CB00023B/3249